LOVE IN THE
ANCIENT WORLD

LOVE IN THE
ANCIENT WORLD

CHRISTOPHER MILES
WITH
JOHN JULIUS NORWICH

PHOTOGRAPHS BY CHRISTOPHER MILES

WEIDENFELD & NICOLSON

First published in Great Britain in 1997
by Weidenfeld & Nicolson

A CIP catalogue record for this book is available
from the British Library
ISBN 0-297-83586-6

Designed by: Peter Butler
Set in: Bembo

Weidenfeld & Nicolson
The Orion Publishing Group Ltd
5 Upper St Martin's Lane
London WC2H 9EA

ENDPAPERS: 'Tomb of the Leopards' in the
Monterozzi cemetery near Tarquinia. In the photo
two leopards in heraldic pose are painted near the
ceiling, while three couples dine on a cushioned
klinai. The women, painted lighter and fair-haired,
could be the wives and not *hetairai*. The woman
on the right is clearly loving to the man next to
her (who is holding up an egg). It was in his
memory that the tomb was probably painted. The
style of the painting is in lively colours and shows
Attic influences. The tomb measures 2.16 metres
high, 3.30 metres wide and 1.70 metres long. *c.*
475 BC. Fondo Lancioni, Tarquinia, Italy.
PAGE 2: Women at Egyptian banquet scene from
the tomb of Nebamun, Thebes. 1400 BC. Ref:
37986 British Museum.
PAGE 3: Limestone relief – *symplegma* figure of
couple making love, from Memphis, Egypt. 2nd
century BC. Petrie Museum, London.
FACING: Bald man client and *hetairai* showing
narrow bed or *kline* with even narrower mattress.
Notice her clothes neatly wrapped, while his are
thrown over a peg. Both show the Greek disregard
for comfort. Drinking cup by the Triptolemos
painter *c.* 470 BC. Ref: ARV 36794. Tarquinia
Museum, Italy.

Contents

Introduction 7

1 *Early Mankind 8*

2 *The Invention of Writing and Laws of Sexual Conduct 22*

3 *The Egyptians 30*

4 *The Minoans and Troy 44*

5 *Gods and Men in Greece 52*

6 *Women in Athens 88*

7 *The Mutilation of the Herms 104*

8 *The Etruscans 110*

9 *The Romans and their Gods 118*

10 *The Women of Rome 130*

11 *The God-Emperor's Scandalous Daughter 140*

12 *The Beginning of the End 152*

Bibliography 172

Acknowledgements 173

Index 174

Introduction

On a scorchingly hot July day in East Africa in 1959, a 46-year-old Englishwoman was searching for bones in the Olduvai Gorge, in what is now Tanzania. She was Mary Leakey, wife of Louis Leakey of the famous family of palaeontologists, and well known as a careful researcher. The midday sun was making it difficult to see bones against the white stones in the sandy soil. Suddenly she saw what seemed to be a bone, not lying down but projecting from the sand. She later wrote, 'It had a hominid look, but the bones seemed enormously thick – too thick surely?' Scraping away the sand she found a massive but undeniably human jawbone. It was from the earliest human species discovered so far, later to be given the scientific name *Zinjanthropus boisei*, and the common one 'Nutcracker man' because of the huge size of the jaw.

In 1978, and after her husband's death, she found some footprints of similar hominids preserved in a layer of volcanic ash at Laetoli, also in Tanzania. This was to prove to an astonished world that mankind had been walking upright three and a half million years ago, a million years earlier than was first thought. But she at once noticed that the footprints consisted of two sets, close together and in step. It seemed that these two remote ancestors of the human race may have been walking arm in arm.

Was it comradeship, friendship or perhaps love, as these two pairs of bare feet walked side by side in Africa so long ago? What do we mean by love? The word has the longest entry of any in the *Oxford Dictionary of Quotations* – though that is hardly surprising for a word which the English language uses so vaguely: in love, making love, loving your friend, loving your dog, loving chocolate. The *Concise Oxford Dictionary* describes love as 'warm affection, attachment, liking or fondness, affectionate devotion ... towards a person or thing'.

We all think we know what we mean by love; yet artists, writers and poets have always found the feeling difficult to express. There is perhaps a universality to attraction: recent experiments have shown that a newborn baby who is shown photographs of good-looking and beautiful faces interspersed with plain ones, remains looking at the more beautiful ones for longer. What people consider attractive does not seem to vary much with time. The beauty of the Egyptian Queen Nefertiti, the golden mask of Tutankhamun, the marble statue of the Venus de Milo and the virile bronze statues of ancient Greek warriors all attract people today. The Greeks already possessed more than one word for love, *eros* for physical love or desire and *agape* for brotherly or spiritual love. But how did we start to define or this most forceful, captivating, infuriating and enjoyable of all emotions?

Hominid footprints, with second smaller set alongside, probably belonging to *Australopithicus afarensis*. The footprints show a well developed arch and no divergence of the big toe as apes. Olduvai Gorge, Laetoli, Tanzania, Africa. This 70 m. trail was found by Mary Leakey in 1978. Photo: John Reader.

7

1 *Early Mankind*

The Cave Dwellers

The anthropologists believe that early man migrated from Africa to Europe about 300,000 years ago. This branch of very early man developed into what are now called Neanderthals and were supposedly a simple folk unable to communicate except by grunts and gestures. However as in Mary Leakey's case of her 'earliest' footprints discovery, anthropological theories are constantly having to be revised as 'earliest dates' are pushed further and further back in time.

The idea of brutish inarticulate Neanderthals sloping from their caves with clubs in their hairy hands has had to be rethought recently. In October 1995 a Slovenian palaeontologist, Dr Ivan Turk, working in a cave in the northwest of his country, found the world's oldest musical instrument, a flute made from a hollowed bone, thought to be 82,000 years old. It was made from the thigh bone of a small bear, and is perforated with holes in a straight alignment on one side.

The only other flute-type instruments so far discovered were made by Homo sapiens, 40,000 years later, who spread across Europe and supplanted the Neanderthals 30,000 years ago. 'If music be the food of love, play on!', as Shakespeare wrote in *Twelfth Night*, feeling that music could be an inspiration for love.

Baudelaire felt that love was only possible when society had reached a certain level of sophistication. In France, at the site at Brassempouy, a beautifully carved woman's head was found, carved on ivory and about 3.5 cm long, indicating this 'certain level of sophistication'. The attraction and simplicity of the sculpted open face, with plaited hair, wide eyes and delicate chin, sums up perhaps the eternal beauty of women from the very earliest times of recorded art. However, it is now thought by Dr Bahn and others that this may be a fake.

However, it certainly moved the Frenchman Edouard Piette; in his 1894 book on *Notes on the History of Primitive Art* he found the work of early man on the whole

RIGHT: Neolithic female statuettes from Grimaldi, Italy. The one on the left is nick-named 'polichinelle' or 'Judy' (as in Punch and Judy), and was found in the grotto of the Prince. Carved from steatite. 6 cm high. The other two were also found in Grimaldi, in the grotto of Baoussé-Roussé. Musée des Antiquités Nationales, St Germain, France.

ABOVE: Palaeolithic female statuette from Fort-Harrouard (Eure-et-Loire), France. Made out of baked clay and probably a divinity from a fertility cult. *c.* 4th millennium. Musée des Antiquités Nationales, St Germain, France.

primitive and savage, but on gazing at this carving he was amazed at the beauty of the woman he called the 'The Lady in the Cowl' (which actually looks more like a snood or coiffure than a cowl), and thought that 'It was love itself that had incited this first sculptor to chisel in ivory this very attractive woman.' Knowing how art has 'progressed' since 1894, this was a brave statement from a Frenchman, who in this case perhaps can avoid the clichéd accusation of the French mind of always being on one track – '*toujours l'amour*'!

In contrast the Venus of Willendorf, who is named after the archaeological site where she was found near the river Danube in Austria, with her bulging thighs, large fecund breasts and distended stomach, cannot today perhaps be described as beauti-ful, nor should present-day Austrians feel any embarrassment at her shape. She was carved in limestone over 26,000 years ago, and was originally thought to be the proof of early man's link with Africa since she could represent the Hottentot female shape in many ways.

Was she a love-object, or was she as some archaeologists would like to call her a 'Goddess of Love', a stone-age Venus?

Recently a small piece of volcanic tuff was found at an Acheulian site at Berekhat Ram in Israel. According to Dr Paul Bahn it has been carbon dated to be between 233,000 and 800,000 years old. On close examination under Alexander Marshack's microscope, small grooves on its 'neck' and 'arms' were detected, clearly indicating that this 'female goddess shape' had been enhanced by human hand. This makes it the world's first man-made 'art' object. Clearly some of the practical tools of early man were artistic creations in themselves, but this tiny piece of volcanic rock serves no practical utilitarian purpose – a big psychological leap from the very practical swallow's nest, however beautiful a creation it is.

Over 200 of these so-called 'Venus figurines' have been found, mostly in caves, from the French Pyrenees to Lake Bikal in Siberia. Unfortunately many were found by chance and their location in the cave was not noted, so the use to which they were put is still not sure. Many archaeologists and pre-historians have often tried to lump these female figurines together, but although they often resemble each other in many ways, they differ in other crucial ones. Not all have extended buttocks or enlarged breasts, and not all have marked vulvas.

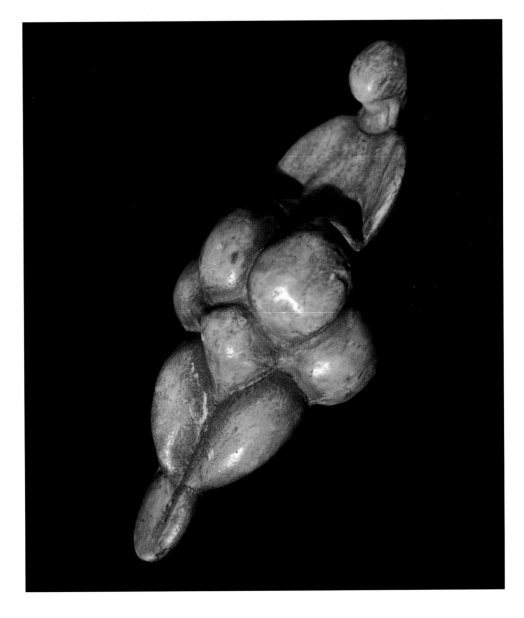

LEFT: 'Venus' of Lespugue, Haute-Garonne, France. Carved from the ivory of a mammoth, the photo is of a restored copy from Dr Paul Bahn's collection as the original is badly broken in the front. *c.* 27,000–16,000 BC. 14.7 cms high. Musée de l'Homme, Paris.

Perhaps the most interesting 'Venus' of all was found in the Haute-Garonne on 9th August 1922 in a cave in Lespuge and is 15cms high. She is carved from the ivory of a mammoth and despite being chipped and broken has an astonishingly modern symbolistic fecund form. Her face is unseen, and small microscopic lines indicate a veil. From her neck down to her buttocks are other thin lines indicating a type of dress, which is very rare for a female figurine of this sort.

Her legs end in a point enabling her to be put upright into the earth, and as she was found among other jumbled artifacts of different ages, so her real place in the cave is not known. However some indication may be learned from a similar shaped figurine found undisturbed in a cave in Russia, where she was found upright in a shallow earth trench under a small roof made from two animal shoulder blades, perhaps indicating some fertility rite to do with the land and/or the woman (or women) of the cave.

To early man large breasts meant a plentiful supply of milk for the child during this last Ice Age. Large hips for child-bearing became more important as symbols of the ideal 'mother' figure in a woman. The idea of what is beautiful changes over the years, and over thousands of years it may be difficult for us to grasp today. Certainly large breasts are more admired nowadays (and in prehistorical times) than they were in ancient Egyptian and Greek times: these little figurines could be the caveman's equivalent of the 'Playboy centrefold'. But clearly above all else they seem to represent the symbol of the female as a source of life.

Also interestingly many of these 'Venuses' were carved contemporary to the many magnificent cave paintings – 99 per cent of which are of animals - and almost none of women, which perhaps again emphasizes their symbolic/religious properties. The few men who were depicted often had animal heads and were perhaps shamans. The cave was both a shelter and religious focus, the womb-like interior could also serve as a sanctuary, or in the cave paintings as a secret area for 'rites of passage' for a young huntsman perhaps with his guide or 'shaman'.

In the famous Lascaux cave complex in south-western France, there are many superb paintings of animals – but in the crypt, where no one is allowed today, and into which it is very difficult to climb down, there is a painting of a huge bison bull which seems to have a spear thrust through its anus and sex organ. A man is lying in front with an erect penis and wearing a bird-like mask. Some feel he is a shaman or witch-doctor. In order to see these paintings a lamp had to be carried with some difficulty deep underground. The journey was perhaps part of an initiation for shamans.

The erect phallus in the Lascaux crypt remains an undeci-phered part of the story, almost certainly religiously symbolic, as are

BELOW: Three breasted statuette, and (right) statuette with phallus, both from Brassempouy, Landes, France. Musée des Antiquités Nationales, St Germain, France. OPPOSITE: 'Venus' of Laussel, Dordogne, France. 54 x 36 cms 22–18,000 BC. Musée d'Aquitaine, France.

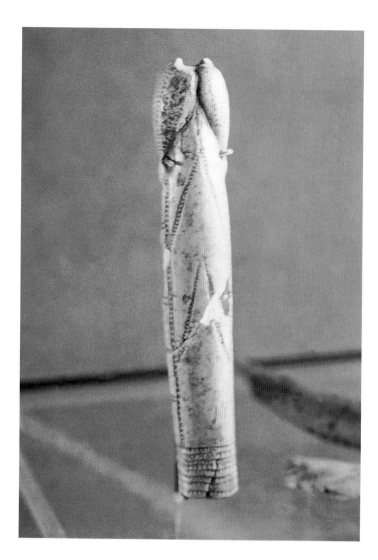

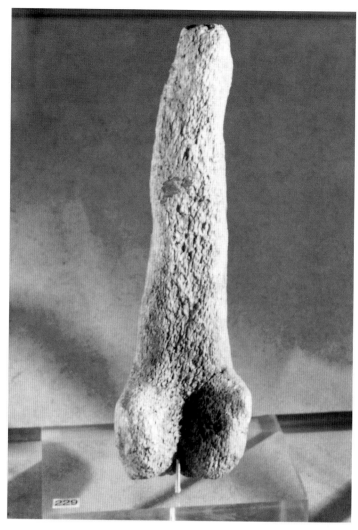

ABOVE: Magdalanian phallus carved in mammoth ivory from Isturitz, Adour, France 17–10,000 BC. The right Magdalanian phallus carved in limestone is from Mas d'Azil, France. 17–10,000 BC. Musée des Antiquités Nationales.

these carved phalluses from the Magdalanian period (17–10,000 BC), one beautifully carved in ivory from Isturitz in the foothills of the Pyrenees, the other in limestone with testicles from Mas d'Azil two hundred miles further east. It has however recently been suggested that they are nothing more symbolic than a dildo!

In some early publications after the First World War it appeared that cave dwellers called Aurignacians, of south-western France, were obsessed by sex, particularly due to the deciphering of the famous Abbé Breuil findings of what he thought were carvings of vulvas all over the cave walls in this region. Abbé Breuil was the man called in to examine the Grotte de Lascaux just after the cave had been discovered by two boys in September 1940. The Abbé called the paintings discovered there 'the Versailles of prehistory'. Recently Dr Paul Bahn has questioned the Abbé's interpretations accused him of 'talking through his beret'; the Abbé even saw the female organ in fishtail motifs carved in the same region. Undeniably some do appear to be vulvas as the one carved on a cave entrance in the Dordogne region of France (30–25,000 BC).

It is, as Bahn points out, remarkably difficult to find examples of the vulva in Palaeolithic art, and 'it is surprisingly hard to find them even among the "Venus" figurines, which were often seen as proof of intense interest in female sexuality; very few have the pubic triangle marked and even fewer have the median cleft.'

The depictions of copulation are also rare, but a scene from a cave wall in Laussel also in the Dordogne, which the French have dubbed 'la carte à jouer' as, like a playing card, it looks the same either way up. In this case the woman is clearly depicted at the bottom of the frame, but whether it is actual copulation taking place is difficult to be sure as the act itself has always posed problems to artists throughout the ages.

As in some recently discovered rain-forest tribes, it is surmised that early man could also have thought that the act of love-making was not the reason for a child appearing nine months later. For them women gave birth alone, and were the supreme mother of the human race – as the earth was mother of their crops.

BELOW: Vulva carved on rock face in a cave in Sergeac, Dordogne, France 30–25,000 BC. Musée des Antiquités Nationales, France.

Also in Laussel an unusual carving was found at the entrance of the cave, 'The Venus with the horn' (*c.* 22–18,000 BC, see p. 16) which was carved in the limestone rock and has been detached for conservation in the nearby museum. As Anne Baring and Jules Cashford point out in their excellent book *The Myth of the Goddess*, she is holding 'in her right hand a bison's horn, crescent-shaped like the moon, notched with the thirteen days of the waxing moon and thirteen months of the lunar year. With her left hand she points to her swelling womb, so creating a connection between the waxing phase of the moon and the fecundity of the human womb.'

The moon, as a symbol of rebirth and physical female cycles, remains an emblem of the goddess of love in the Mediterranean world right up to the time of

RIGHT: 'La carte à jouer'. Dordogne, France. Musée d'Aquitaine, France.

Christ, as this relief of Aphrodite, the Greek goddess of love clearly shows with its marble crescent moon clearly carved behind her.

There are no known depictions of men, women and children together until the Bronze Age 5,000 years later, and even these are extremely rare. In Alta in Norway there are rock carvings of what appear to be adults and children, but the larger figures could equally well denote people of a higher standing than the smaller ones. However in Russia, Dimitri Cheremisin has recently found some petroglyphs in the remote valley in the mountains of South Altai which are from roughly the same time in the Bronze Age (c. 3,000 BC) and show a man and a woman standing together with linked hands. The woman appears to have a child (maybe as yet unborn) between her thighs.

ABOVE: Aphrodite with crescent moon carved in marble. Hellenistic c. 25 BC. Carved as one of the many panels made for the huge colonnaded monument named the 'Sebasteion', which was built in honour of the Roman Emperor Caesar–Augustus (Sebastos in Greek) and his Julio–Claudian successors. Aphrodisias – city of Aphrodite, Turkey.

RIGHT: Carvings of a man and woman on a rock face in Chadyr near the Ukok mountain range in Russia. Width 80 cms and height 1m 20. Probably made in the Bronze Age. The drawing below shows the figures themselves, just visible on the rock face.

They are called 'the family of Chadyr', named after the little valley in which they were found. In the local ancient Altai language the word 'Chady' means 'habitation', which could indicate that there was an ancient dwelling place there even as far back as 5,000 years. Dimitri Cheremisin wonders if they are just an engraving of an ordinary family of our far off ancestors, or are they mythological archetypes representing a grander and more generalized idea?

In the end, however, he came to the conclusion that what the artist was trying to express was 'love'.

The Megalith Makers

Almost at the same time these petroglyphs were being made work began on one of the world's largest megalith sites – Stonehenge in southern England. Only recently has accurate scientific dating been possible with the Radio Carbon Accelerator, sometimes to within 18 years. The outer ditch was once thought to have taken hundreds of years to build, whereas in fact it took only fifty. This shows us that those responsible must have lived in a much more structured and ordered society than originally thought. The great stones arrived from Wales in about 2660 BC, at the same time as the building of the first pyramids in Egypt.

There are new theories that Stonehenge did have a connection with the Earth Mother goddess, and we do know it was used as an astrological machine which, among other things, could predict and calculate the moon's phases and eclipses. The moon, as we have seen, was one of the earliest symbols of the Mother goddess.

Another great neolithic monument, Silbury Hill, was started at about this time. The structure is the largest man-made mound in Europe, and according to researches carried out by Michael Dames, this enormous fecund hill is in the shape of the great goddess herself, which he suggests is formed from the reflection of the moon on the surrounding lake, which mysteriously fills up every two years or so. The project would have taken 400 people, working ten hours a day, ten years to complete! As the early builders reinforced their work with chalk walls, the hill would have appeared

BELOW: Silbury Hill photographed three-quarters of a mile away from the sarsen stone by the entrance to West Kennet Long Barrow. This man-made hill is about 130 feet high, and the base is 550 feet in diameter. It covers an area of 5.5 acres. *c* 2,500 BC. Near Avebury, Wiltshire, England.

RIGHT: West Kennet Long Barrow looking from the inside towards the opening which faces east, probably for rites involving the sun entering the chamber at the winter solstice. It is the largest burial mound in England (340 feet long). During excavations in 1955 twenty skeletons were found on the floor from the neolithic period, *c.* 2,500 BC. Near Avebury, Wiltshire, England.

ABOVE: Cerne Abbas Giant is over 180 feet long, and an enclosed field near the feet of the giant known as the Frying-pan or Ring, was the site of the May Day Maypole dance rite. Cerne Abbas, Dorset, England.

like a gleaming white pyramid. The fact that after several major excavations (even the great Egyptologist Sir Flinders Petrie undertook some digging in 1922), nothing has been found in the centre of the great hill — which only adds to the mystery of the hill's purpose. A procession of worshippers may have come along the long avenue of stones from the great circle nearby at Avebury, whose vast stones dwarf the Wiltshire village which has since impudently sprung up in its middle, and made their way to the top of the hill for some ceremony for the 'goddess'.

Dr George Meaden disagrees with this theory, but he does agree that the hill is certainly man-made and in honour of the 'Mother-Goddess'. His reasons, though, are very different. He feels that early man was greatly influenced by divine-like phenomena, such as lightning, storms and whirlwinds. The latter often appeared as a spout from the sky which hit the earth in a circular shaped impact — this phallic shaped spout was seen as the sky-god impregnating the earth mother-goddess. The shape left by this moment of impact was often a clearly defined circle. As man had already started farming by this time, this could well have happened in a field of corn.

The area of 'divine impregnation' when the moment the sky-god made love to the earth-goddess became sacred and was marked out by wooden posts. These in their turn were supplemented by standing stones ... and the reason for the 'sacred sites' of stone circles was born. It seems that early humans were more aware of earth as a living organism than we are today. Even in the early religions the earth was referred to as a 'she' or 'thou', and in many languages is still a 'she'. The mother-earth-goddess, as we have seen, was the supreme being at the start of the social awareness in the human race, but after the Bronze Age we see a change of supremacy in most societies from the female to the male – from the receptive womb of the mother to the often aggressive war-like phallic male.

Nowhere is this phallic warrior male more evident than above the little village of Cerne Abbas in Dorset, England, where carved into the chalk hill is the ancient Cerne Abbas Giant. His 26ft long phallus carved into the chalk of the hill makes it the biggest in prehistory! Some think that the club he is wielding was added later by the Romans to turn him into their hero Hercules. If the club was carved at the same time as the giant it would make him Roman and not prehistoric, and academics are still divided on this issue. Many couples have spent the night camped out on his penis to help them conceive. The present Marquess of Bath, after trying in vain to start a family, visited the giant with his second wife Virginia and the old pagan rite worked with the marchioness. She duly conceived nine months later and called her newborn daughter – Sylvie Cerne.

Studies have clearly shown that where plough agriculture is practised and animals kept on a large scale, most of the agricultural work is done by men. Women who had helped forage for food, now helped in the house, and man became dominant in most societies as ownership of the house, animals and land became important. The woman then became as much his chattel as the beasts he herded.

BELOW: Part of Avebury stone circle and earth-works, which cover a site of 28 acres. The top of the bank of the ditch originally rose to about 55 feet, which makes it one of the greatest prehistoric sites in Europe. The moon-queen Ave or Avu presided over the two sites of Avebury and Silbury. On the horizon can be seen the standing stones which begin the West Kennet Avenue leading to the Sanctuary (destroyed in the 18th cent.) Avebury, Wiltshire, England.

2 The Invention of Writing and Laws of Sexual Conduct

With the invention of writing in around 3100 BC in Mesopotamia, now Iraq, mankind took its first real step forward towards modern civilization, and we learn with more clarity for the first time in the history of the human race what people were actually doing in their lives and what they thought about their past. These early myths of the creation of the world and the formation of their own gods reflect the efforts of men and women in coming to terms with their own sexuality and the wonder of birth and fear of death.

We also learn of more earthly matters, such as the large lists for the palace store houses and even of the first written marriage contracts.

Now that large cities were being built, and farming techniques were being refined by men, the role of women was beginning to change and diminish. However at this time women were still able to have more than one husband – a throw-back to earlier Bronze Age times. Eight hundred years after the first writing appeared, however, the Babylonian king, Urukagina, put an end to this age-old custom of 'polyandry'. So the traditional role of women as mothers and house-keepers gained in importance as their lives outside the home became more restricted.

Babylonian creation myths were adapted as the role of women declined. In the later myth Tiamat, the salt-water ocean, tries to avenge the murder of Apsu, the sweet

RIGHT: The carving at the top of the black basalt stele shows King Hammurabi of Babylon with his right hand extended holding a scroll of his laws. These codes were very advanced as they recognized no blood feuds, private retribution or marriage by capture. They even stated that a barren wife might legally give her husband a handmaid to bear children, reflecting concern with our contemporary dilemma over surrogacy and artificial insemination. Louvre Museum, Paris.

ocean, and she is in turn killed and divided by Marduk, the male god chosen by the the gods collectively to be their champion. Marduk splits Tiamat's remains, and makes half her body into the sky and the other half the earth. The creation of the universe thus became a masculine event.

Women's new role and the new social order were laid down in the first known list of laws by King Hammurabi of Babylon (1792–1750 BC). They were carved on this black basalt stele, now in the Louvre in Paris. Of the 282 laws, 57 are to do with marriage and sexual conduct, such as the law which demanded that 'if a wife was barren she should provide her husband with a substitute child bearer'.

Marriages were arranged by the parents. But one law, number 156, seems to hint at love at the end – 'if a father has betrothed a bride to his son and the father has already lain in her breasts, he shall pay half a "mina" of silver and return all that she brought from her father's house, so that she may marry the husband of her heart' – on the whole, though, love did not get much of a look in.

Where love did get a look in was at the Babylonian temple of the goddess of love, Ishtar, in Sumer, as the Greek historian Herodotus reported:

There is a very shameful custom in which every woman of the city has to go once in her life to the temple of Innana and give herself to a strange man. The rich ladies drive to the temple in covered carriages with many servants, most of the women sit in the precinct of the temple with plaited string around their head. They all sit in rows, with gangways in between so the men can walk through and make their choice. Once a woman has taken her seat she is not allowed to go home until a man has thrown a silver coin into her lap and taken her outside to lie with her. It does not matter what value it is, because once the coin is thrown it becomes sacred to the goddess and cannot be refused. Tall handsome women soon manage to get home again, but the ugly ones stay a long time before they can fulfil the law, some even as long as four years.

BELOW: Relief showing Babylonian or Chaldean women, captured during an Assyrian campaign, in the camp. Assyrian 645–635 BC from Nineveh, North Palace. Ref: WA 134386, British Museum, London.

ABOVE: Etching by Suzy Miles of a statue of the goddess Aphrodite. Her two most important emblems can be seen: the upturned crescent moon on her bust, and the evening star on her head-dress. This bust used to adorn the facade of the theatre of Aphrodisias, the Hellenistic city of Aphrodite, from where the goddess looked down on her audience. Statue 2nd century. AD. Aphrodisias, Turkey.

By calling it 'shameful', it is clear that Herodotus, by the time he wrote (*c.* 450 BC), had lost touch with the idea of sex as a sacrament, which is odd because there were many temple prostitutes to the Greek goddess of love – Aphrodite – during his own lifetime, especially in the busy port of Corinth, but perhaps even these had lost the true original meaning of the sacrament of sex by this time.

Certainly it is a difficult concept for us to grasp today, but the goddess of love and regeneration was also the 'mother' who succours and helps, and who also bestows fertility. The same goddess could represent both virginity and fulfilment – both mother and prostitute and this double image was also represented by the dark and bright phases of the moon, the symbol of the goddess of love, wherever she was to be found in the Mediterranean area.

North of Babylon in Mesopotamia, was the great Hittite Empire, whose written language evolved mostly on its own and remains the earliest record of the Indo-European languages – 'kardi' to the heart – 'cordi' in Latin: kuis? – who? in Latin 'quis'?

Early Hittite tablets survive today, found in a city whose remains still stand untouched by tourism high up in the Anatolian plain – Bogazköy. Nearby is the sacred site of Yazilikaya where, high in a mountain valley, the main gods and goddesses can still be seen carved on the rock face. To the Hittites a foreign god was not considered an enemy or a rival, but was absorbed in their own pantheon, so that its efficacy could be put to the common good.

This tolerance reflects the Hittite attitude towards their own laws of moral behaviour, which differed to the Jewish ones of Yahweh mentioned later on in this chapter. The Hittites had a dignified and enlightened attitude to human life. The death penalty was sparingly used, only in the case of serious offences against the state, incest and:

> 'If a man does evil with a woman in the mountains who is not his wife, he shall be punished by death.
> If a man does evil with a head of cattle, he shall be punished by death.
> If a man does evil with a sheep, he shall be punished by death.
> If anyone does evil with a pig, he shall be punished by death.
> If a man does evil with a horse or mule, there shall be no punishment.
> If an ox leaps at a man, the ox shall die, but the man shall not die. A sheep may be offered up instead of the man and they shall kill that.
> If a pig leaps at a man, there shall be no punishment.'

The refusal to punish a man (and the animal) who has done evil with a horse or mule probably refers back to the reverence of more ancient Indo-European peoples for the horse and the ancient custom of the 'horse sacrifice'. Somewhat gratifying to note that neither the pig nor the man will be punished, even if the pig 'leaps at a man'!

The Monotheistic God of the Chosen Race

Two hundred miles south of Babylon is the city of Ur, where Abraham and his people were living and who left for southern Israel at the time of the laws of King Hammurabi. They left because of the calling of their God, Yahweh, who told them to search for another land in the south. So Abraham descended into Palestine, arriving at Hebron.

The male god Yahweh of the Old Testament was for the Israelites the one and only god. For in Palestine, where the fertile land had been fought over by the heads of tribes for thousands of years, the male warrior god naturally ruled supreme.

For the Hebrew priests the possibility of having another god, or even for their own god Yahweh to marry, was totally unthinkable. Having an only all powerful single god left little room for manoeuvre or feminine influence. So there remained no dialogue between the patriarchal and matriarchal visions of life. What Yahweh said, or what the male prophets and priests said on his behalf, was the unquestioned law and religion.

In Judaism the creation of the universe and first human was an all-male event. Yahweh first created man from the dust of the earth and while Adam was sleeping took one of his ribs which he then made into a woman.

ABOVE: Relief showing Babylonian or Chaldean women, captured during an Assyrian campaign, as they sit in the camp. Assyrian 645–635 BC from Nineveh, North Palace. Ref: WA 124919 British Museum, London.

ABOVE: Relief showing Assyrian forces pursuing Arabs – the Assyrians who are on foot and in chariots chase the Arabs on camels and also on foot. Assyrian 645–635 BC. From the North Palace, Nineveh. Ref: WA 124925. British Museum, London.

Artists throughout the ages have had difficulty in portraying this all–male virgin birth, as in the Judaic story of creation women are not a part of it, again reflecting their sexual attitudes and the status of women in their society.

Adam then said 'this is now bone of my bones and shall be called Wo-man, because she was taken out of man. They were both naked and unashamed in the garden of Eden.'

Yahweh then told the woman 'Ye shall not eat of the tree in the middle of the garden', but there was a snake who beguiled the woman and she did eat of the forbidden fruit. She also gave her husband to eat, and their eyes were opened and they knew that they were naked, and sewed aprons of fig leaves together. Yahweh later discovers this and curses the snake for ever more, and then makes the woman give birth in sorrow and man to rule over her.

This concept of Original Sin holds woman to be the cause of man's fall. She became associated with the temptations and the evils of the flesh, and responsible for the bringing into the world of suffering and sin. This image of woman has determined men's attitude to her in the western world ever since.

The patriarchal system was so established that by the time of King Solomon, who ruled for twenty years from 935 BC, polygamy was common. Solomon himself had 700 wives and 300 concubines!

The most intriguing story of Solomon concerns the Queen of Sheba who came to test his wisdom. She arrived with a great train of camels with gold, spices and precious stones and was much impressed by Solomon and all his glory. Sheba came from the voluptuous Orient and represents sensuality and the exotic, and her encounter with Solomon is often shown as a battle of the sexes as well as of the wits. All the Old Testament says of their meeting is that 'King Solomon gave unto the queen of Sheba all her desire, whatsoever she asked.'

The Queen of Sheba is one of a long line of biblical seductresses, including Delilah and Jezebel, who represent all the Israelites feared – exotic, erotic, foreign and female. Delilah betrayed Samson, the great Israelite hero, by seducing him into revealing that the source of his great strength lay in his uncut hair. Once she has cut it, the weakened Samson was captured by the Philistines.

The prophet Ezekiel gives the prostitute or harlot a hateful tirade, aimed mainly at the inhabitants of Jerusalem, who like Solomon, lived in what was then a wicked city.

'And the word of the Lord came to Ezekiel saying: Set thy face towards Jerusalem and prophesy against the land of Israel for there are women who committed whoredoms and doted on their neighbours, all of them desirable young men riding upon horses . . . She doted on their paramours, whose members were as the members of asses and whose issue is like the issue of horses. And the company shall stone them with stones and dispatch them with swords – thus will I cause lewdness to cease.'

Sexual deviations of any sort were forbidden by pain of death. 'The Lord hath said to the children of Israel – "If a man lies with a man, as with a woman, both of them have committed an abomination; they shall be put to death, their blood is upon them. If a man lies with a beast, he shall be put to death; and you shall kill the beast. If a woman approaches any beast and lies with it, you shall kill the woman and the beast."'

Abraham had continued his journey from Hebron into northern Egypt for better grazing. Once in Egypt he marries his half sister Sarah, but although she bears him one child, Isaac, in old age, whe also in true Babylonian style offers Abraham a concubine, Hagar, by whom Abraham has other children. Once in Egypt the Israelites were enslaved by the Pharaohs, but many years later, Joseph, a descendant of Abraham secures himself a prominent position in the court of the Pharaohs. Later, and after Yahweh has plagued the Egyptian army, their new leader Moses is able to lead a mass exodus of the Israelites out of Egypt with the Ark of Covenant. When the Israelites left Egypt they took with them the ritual of circumcision, which was practised there on adolescent boys, as can be seen in the tomb wall carving of 2300 BC. It was neither universal nor compulsory in Egypt, as it was in Israel, where it was an article of the Jewish faith.

3 The Egyptians

The huge pyramids and the massive, forbidding architecture of the ancient Egyptians hardly suggest that their makers had much time for love and sex. But when we decipher their inscriptions on stone and their documents on papyrus, we find a very different world. It is still a world known only to a few, for most of these texts were translated in the early 20th century, when the tide of Victorian prudery was only just beginning to recede. Many of the Egyptian tomb reliefs and mythological stories were considered too shocking to publish.

Gods and Goddesses

To understand a people, it is often best to begin by understanding their religion. In the Egyptian myth of creation the first of the gods, the sun god Atum created himself from primordial matter. Then he was masturbated by the 'divine hand' and his seed formed the next two deities, Shu the god of air, and Tefenet the goddess of moisture. The 'divine hand' is a complex idea, in that Atum remains the only god at this moment and the apparition of the divine hand was somehow due to the intervention of the goddess Hathor. In the ancient daily rites for the god Atum at Karnak, the priestess of the temple reenacted this creation ritual with a large ithyphallic statue of Atum.

Hathor and Atum produced two children, Nut, the sky, and Geb, the earth, shown together in this papyrus from a book of the dead in the British Museum. Nut and Geb then bore four further children, Isis, Osiris, Seth and Nephthys.

Was there an Egyptian goddess of love? The nearest to such a being was Hathor, sometimes depicted with a cow's

30

TOP: The ceiling of Hathor's temple at Dendarah, showing ancient colour. The goddess Nut, shaped as a thin long-bodied woman in the lower half of the picture, here ejects the sun god Ra from her vulva.
ABOVE: Ivory clappers, used in temple music making in rituals, probably for the goddess of love, Hathor, personified as the divine hand (p. 30). Petrie Museum, London.

head, sometimes with a human one. In either case she generally has cow's ears and a large bouffant wig. Her 'divine hand' aspect was symbolized by a pair of hand-shaped ivory 'clappers', which were banged together to a musical accompaniment in the temples dedicated to her.

Another goddess associated with Hathor (her daughter) was Isis, who is also portrayed with the horns of a cow. Her worship was later adopted by the Greeks and then the Romans, and the cult continued in Italy until 500 years after Christ. She married her brother Osiris, god of fertility, and had a child called Horus. In ancient Egypt, at least in royal circles, it was quite usual for a sister and brother to marry. Horus succeeded his father Osiris as 'Lord of all Egypt', and was worshipped throughout the land. Nearly always represented with the head of a falcon, he became the new sky god, replacing Nut.

Horus later had a quarrel with his brother Seth, god of disorder and confusion. A papyrus from the Middle Kingdom, dating from about 1900 BC, includes the only known homosexual passage from that era, describing how Seth tried to seduce Horus. 'The divine person of Seth said to the divine person of Horus, "How beautiful are your buttocks, how vital!"' Later in the story, 'Seth said to Horus, "Come let us spend a pleasant hour at my house." Horus answered, "With pleasure, with pleasure." When it was evening a bed was spread for them and they lay down. During the night Seth made his penis stiff and placed it between the loins of Horus. Horus put his hands between his loins and caught the sperm of Seth.' Horus told his mother Isis what had happened, and she, as his magical helper, made him ejaculate into a jar, which she then emptied over Seth's favourite vegetable, lettuce. When Seth ate the lettuce, Horus' sperm entered him and (perhaps fittingly for a god of confusion) he became pregnant. Later both Horus and Seth stood in front of the god Thoth, 'lord of the divine words', and Seth admitted to having behaved aggressively towards Horus. Thoth ordered the seed to come out of Seth; it emerged in the shape of a golden disc, which Thoth took and placed on his own head saying, 'Horus is in the right, and Seth is in the wrong.' Seth was angry and vowed revenge.

BELOW: Panel on the south wall of the Roman Mammisi in the Dendarah complex. The goddess Hathor is shown with her child Ihy and Amun as the father. Emperor Trajan built this during Roman times; the rites to Hathor had changed by then, so it has a sanctuary of two long rooms where the ceremonies were carried out, away from the public's profane gaze.

The Sexual Conduct of the Pharaohs

The pharaoh was also a god, seen as the son of the supreme deity Amun-Re and an earthly form of the sun god Horus. He was responsible not only for civil law and order but for the good fortune of Egypt. Since that included a successful harvest, he was considered the divine regulator of the annual flooding of the Nile.

To keep the royal family free of outsiders, and to strengthen its claim to the throne, pharaohs often married their half-sisters, sometimes even their mothers and real sisters. These incestuous marriages were often childless, and such children as there were tended to be stillborn; if they lived, they were usually daughters. This gave additional importance to the female line, and occasionally a woman even reigned as pharaoh. The most famous of these was the great Queen Hatshepsut, who ruled from 1503 to 1482 BC. Since there was no concept of a female ruler in Egyptian tradition she had to be described and portrayed as a man, even to the extent of wearing a false beard. To validate her claim to the throne she maintained that she was born of the god Amun; she was therefore obliged to rewrite history (or mythology), describing how Amun had seduced her mother, the Queen Ahmosis, wife of

Tuthmosis I. Her story, in which the god disguised himself as Tuthmosis and entered her mother's bed-chamber, is told in the inscriptions on the walls of her temple at Deir al-Bahari in Upper Egypt.

> 'Amun found the queen in the inner rooms of the palace. Smelling his divine scent, she woke up and smiled at him. At once he proceeded towards her. He lusted after her, and gave her his heart. He allowed her to see him in his real god's figure, having come close to her. She rejoiced at his virility and said, 'How splendid it is to see you face to face. Your divine strength engulfs me, your dew runs all through my limbs!' The god did once more what he wished with her and said, 'Truly, Hatshepsut will be the name of the child I have placed in your belly.'

The tomb was not merely a monument to dynastic claims, but also the place where the body was prepared for the afterlife. The mummified body had to be given back all the faculties it had used during life, especially sexual vigour, and was often equipped with nipples or a phallus of gold. In the great pyramid of Giza the pharaoh underwent an extraordinary last sexual rite in order to complete his duties on earth

OPPOSITE ABOVE: Bronze statuette of the goddess Isis who holds her child Horus in her arms (see p. 32). Petrie Museum, London.
OPPOSITE BELOW: Part of the wall in the Room of Hatshepsut, which was walled up by the pharaoh Tuthmosis lll at Karnak, Egypt. He tried to erase the cartouches of Queen/Pharaoh Hatshepsut, whose chiselled figure in the centre is being purified by the gods Horus on her left and Thoth on her right.
ABOVE: Mortuary Temple of Hatshepsut in Deir al-Bahri in the Theban Hills, Egypt. This extraordinary temple was designed by Hatshepsut's architect Senenmut and took eight years to build from about 1435 BC, but it is not known if she was buried there. The Second Colonnade tells the story of her birth.

and to the gods. His dead body was aligned with one of the long channels made in the pyramid wall, through which the star Sirius could be seen. Sirius was the embodiment of the goddess Isis, and the pharaoh was the embodiment of Horus. So to continue the pharaoh's line his mummified body, with an erect penis pointing towards the channel and the star, had to impregnate the goddess at the exact moment the star rose and could be seen through the channel. Nine and a half months later the star rose again on the other side of the pyramid – a sign of the rebirth of the god and the continuation of the pharaonic line.

One of the most interesting pharaohs was Akhenaten, who came to the throne in 1375 BC. Son of Amenhotep III and named after him, he changed his name as he rebelled against his father and all that he stood for. He assumed the office of the high priest of Aten, a new conception of the all-powerful sun god Amun, whose priests became the most powerful in Egypt. He then declared himself the one and only god and erased his father's names from the temples and palace of Thebes.

Akhenaten went on to obliterate the names of all the other Egyptian gods and closed their temples – a vast undertaking which must have called for military force. He incorporated the symbol of the god Aten into the pharaoh's formal written name, and became the world's first human head of a monotheistic religion. He moved his palace from Thebes and created his own city at el-'Amarna, also undertaking a huge building programme in Karnak, where there are the remains of colossal statues of himself and Queen Nefertiti. He is regularly depicted with large feminine lips and swelling hips and belly, and some Egyptologists have suggested that he may have been physically abnormal. Others believe that he was trying to personify a hermaphrodite god – in which case, however, the complete absence of breasts remains a mystery.

Akhenaten's first wife was his mother Tiy, by whom he had a daughter. Next he married a maternal cousin, the ravishing Nefertiti – whose painted bust, now in Berlin, still stands as an example of supreme female beauty. By her he had three more daughters. He seems to have deeply loved her and his children, breaking a 2000-year-old tradition by appearing in public with them. His third and fourth wives – to whom he was not related – each bore him a son, and his fifth was his daughter by Nefertiti. It was his elder son who succeeded him: the celebrated Tutankhamun, the

OPPOSITE: The Eighth Pylon at Karnak was built by Queen Hatshepsut but was altered by Akhenaten, who erased the name of Amun.
ABOVE LEFT: A statue of the pharaoh Akhenaten. Cairo Museum.
TOP: Akhenaten and Nefertiti seated with their daughters under the rays of the sun god Aten. Cairo Museum.
ABOVE: Akhenaten with raised arms in an act of worship. Cairo Museum.

treasures from whose tomb are famous throughout the world. This tomb – the only known royal tomb of the New Kingdom never to have been robbed or desecrated – was discovered in 1922 by the British archaeologist Howard Carter, in the course of excavations sponsored by the Earl of Carnarvon.

Akhenaten's strange life was later to be the inspiration of what are known as the Theban plays by the Athenian playwright Sophocles, in which he is transformed into the tragic King Oedipus. The parallels between the two stories are indeed striking: both Akhenaten and Oedipus had mystic encounters with sphinxes, in cities called Thebes; both received predictions of death; both – demonstrating what Sigmund Freud was later to describe as the 'Oedipus complex' – married their mothers; both were ultimately deposed by their own sons and sent into exile.

People and Everyday Life

The myths of the Egyptian gods formed part of a royal state religion with its own priests, priestesses and huge temples. The general public was however excluded from all religious ceremonies. The people therefore had their own more personal and local deities, who provided a fertile field for superstitions of all kinds. Vast quantities of

ABOVE: Greek marble sphinx from a grave in Corinth. *c.* 550 BC. Corinth Archaeological Museum, Greece.
RIGHT: Stone relief of couple with arm around the neck from the tomb of Queen Mentuhopte II. Ref: AS 1621. Egyptian Museum, Munich.

documents written on papyrus, fortunately preserved by the dry heat of the climate, have provided much valuable information about the lives – and even the feelings – of the ordinary Egyptians. We now know, for example, that incestuous marriages were not the exclusive province of the pharaohs: many letters between husbands and wives are addressed to 'my dear brother' or 'dearest sister', appellations which were formerly assumed to be nothing more than conventional greetings, but have since been revealed to mean exactly what they say. Why such marriages were so popular remains a mystery; but the Egyptians clearly attached much importance to questions of family and descent, and in view of the number of different races and tribes inhabiting the Nile Valley, it may well have been believed that an incestuous marriage would strengthen the family's social standing.

Unlike their counterparts in ancient Greece, Egyptian women had the right to act on their own behalf in marriage agreements. Weddings were great occasions for those who could afford them, as is shown by a letter from a couple prevented by illness from attending one: 'There are not many roses yet as they are in short supply, and from all the estates and makers of garlands we could only just scrape together the thousand we have sent you ... We had as many narcissi as we wanted, so instead of the two thousand you asked for we have sent four thousand ... We look on these young people as our own, and esteem and love them even more.'

ABOVE: Two men and a woman at table with unusual interlocking arms, attended by a servant girl. This funereal stele was commissioned by Amenemhet. Probably the Intermediate Period *c.* 2,100 BC. Cairo Museum.

ABOVE: Dancing and musician girls. 5th dynasty, *c.* 2,600 BC, from the Tomb of Nakht at Thebes.

OPPOSITE TOP: Terracotta figurine of a concubine. Her wide hips and exaggerated pubic region, small high breasts and elaborate hair-do – and also perhaps the fact that she cannot stand upright – typify Egyptian attitudes to the female sex. She was probably deposited in a shrine. *c.* 1500 BC. Petrie Museum, London.

OPPOSITE BELOW: Serving girl at a banquet, standing by laden tables of fruit and food. Scene from the tomb of Nebamun at Thebes. *c.* 1400 BC. Ref: 37986. British Museum.

Successful marriages seldom leave their mark on history; it is the divorces that are more likely to be documented. The oldest divorce document so far discovered in the world dates from about 1200 BC, and is between a woman named Hunero and her husband Hesi Senebef, who brought the action against her. It is written on limestone in hieratic script, a simplified form of hieroglyphs. It gives no reason for their divorce, but specifies how the couple's property was to be divided, with Hunero's dowry being returned to her family.

Contraception and Extramarital Attitudes

The use of contraceptives was known; one of the earliest methods, described in the Kahun papyrus, was to mix crocodile dung into a paste, which was made into a sort of tampon and inserted into the vagina. Another, perhaps understandably more common method was to make a similar tampon with honey. (Such a device was said to have been used 3,000 years later by the film star Mae West.) Scientific experiments have shown that honey is in fact a mild spermicide.

Love and sex outside marriage, apart from the usual extramarital affairs, were made easier in two ways: by prostitutes, and by certain festivals. When Herodotus, the Greek explorer and historian of the 5th century BC, visited Egypt and wrote accounts of all he heard and saw, he mentioned a festival in honour of Hathor, goddess of love, at Bubastis, the modern Zagazig:

'When the pilgrims go to Bubastis they go by river, men and women together, a great number in every boat. Some of the women make a noise with clappers, while others play pipes or sing. When they draw up beside a town some of the women dance, while others stand up in the boat and expose their genitals.'

Hathor's main temple was at Dendarah on the Nile; here the goddess of love and music was served by an entourage of female musicians and dancers. They used

BELOW: Ramesses III making offerings to the gods with his wife and children at Karnak.
RIGHT: The dress of beads from the Petrie Museum. Recent skeletal finds indicate that it would have fitted an adult Egyptian woman.
OPPOSITE: Columns in the Great Hypostyle Hall at Karnak, Egypt. This immense hall consists of 134 columns many of which are 23 metres high with papyrus-bud capitals. The cartouches shown here at the base of the columns are mostly by Ramesses II and are dedicated to the god Amun. The whole colonnaded area covers an astonishing 6,000 square metres.

percussion instruments in the main, including tambourines and a sistrum, a rattle suspended on two hoops. Many of the temple musicians would have been from the richer classes and unpaid.

At the Petrie Museum, a dress has been recently recreated from a pile of glazed beads. One of only two examples to have survived even in part from the ancient world, it dates from about 2400 BC. It was obviously designed less to conceal than to reveal: one has only to look at the breast caps with their delicately-shaded nipples and at the way the whole fabric is weighted by numbers of shells – which, being associated with the vulva, give it added erotic significance. Each shell contains a small pebble, so that it would have tinkled suggestively when the wearer moved. It would probably have been worn for some ritual by a temple dancer, for the purpose of channelling the sexual power of some female divinity such as the goddess Hathor.

4 The Minoans and Troy

By the time of Herodotus, the once-magnificent royal palace of Knossos in Crete had already lain buried for a thousand years, victim of two major earthquakes. Only in 1900 did the British archaeologist Sir Arthur Evans begin serious excavations, not only uncovering but restoring a considerable part of the building. Among his finds was a Minoan goddess, made in faience around 1600 BC. She holds a snake in each hand, has a lion cub on her head, and her clothes are decorated with birds and bees. Her bodice is open, exposing her breasts – perhaps to emphasize her function as the giver and nurturer of life. The frescoes in the palace – at least in Evans's imaginative reconstructions – demonstrate clearly enough the vitality of the Minoans themselves, not least in the superb portrayal of leaping dolphins. They also illustrate the contemporary ideals of feminine beauty. The stucco relief of the 'Priest-King' with his tiny waist and swaggering walk, contrasts memorably with the beautiful face of a Minoan woman – probably a priestess – whom Evans named 'La Parisienne' because of her painted lips and elaborate coiffure.

The most famous priestess of all was Ariadne, daughter of King Minos of Crete, who in the Cretan myth helped Theseus, son of the king of Athens, find and kill the man-eating bull-headed Minotaur in the labyrinth beneath the Palace. She gave him a ball of thread, which he reeled out behind him so that after killing the monster he could find his way back. In the earliest versions of the story Ariadne

was goddess of vegetation in pre-Minoan Crete, and she therefore had two personas: the gloomy, autumnal and dying one, honoured with gloomy sacrificial rites, and the cheerful, springlike and renewing one, celebrated with a joyful festival. Later, however, the classical Greeks changed the emphasis of the legend to create the story familiar to us today – underlining the importance of the male in society and the growing power of the masculine in the Mediterranean world. The vase on p. 49 shows a charming depiction of love between Theseus and Ariadne, holding hands as he gently strokes her chin.

In later Cretan society there grew up a strong military tradition. The historian Ephorus mentions a puberty ritual in which a young Cretan boy would be carried off by a male lover to some rural retreat for two months. After this initiation the couple would return to the city, where the boy would be given the equivalent of a military uniform, a drinking cup and a bull, which he would be expected to sacrifice; he would be regarded thereafter with greatly increased respect.

OPPOSITE: Wall fresco of the 'Prince of the Lilies'. This was found at the end of the corridor leading into the Central Court. He wears a crown of lilies from which sprout peacock plumes and a large lock of hair falls down over his breast and beneath his clenched right hand. *c.* 1550 BC. Herakleion Museum, Crete.

ABOVE: The Throne Room at Knossos. The throne, which is made of gypsum, was found and left in exactly the same place as it is today. The walls of two flanking griffins and flowers are copies of the original frescoes found there. *c.* 1550 BC. Knossos.

The Minoans exercised an important influence on mainland Greece, especially in their love of luxury. There is, for example, a bath in the Minoan style in what remains of the Queen's bathroom in the palace of King Nestor near Pylos in the Peloponnese. Not far away, near Mycenae, a fresco was discovered of a voluptuous woman; painted about 1400 BC, it again shows a strong Minoan influence (see p. 49). With it was found a small ivory group of goddesses and a child (see p. 50). They sit embracing each other, in flounced dresses under a single cloak, while the child climbs down from the lap of one of the goddesses. This lovely piece, which seems to radiate love and contentment, may well depict the 'two queens and a young god' mentioned on certain tablets found near Nestor's palace.

Helen of Troy

It was from the bay at Sphacteria near Pylos that King Nestor set out with ninety ships for Troy, to participate in that epic war which, according to legend, resulted from the most fateful love affair of antiquity: that of Paris, son of King Priam of Troy, and Helen, the wife of King Menelaus of Sparta. Paris abducted Helen – 'the face

ABOVE: Bull's head from the Little Palace of Knossos. The head is in fact a rhyton, or drinking vessel, but was probably used for libations. The magnificent head is carved from a solid block of black steatite, with eyes of inlaid rock crystal and jasper with nostrils made of mother of pearl. The horns are made of gilded wood. *c.* 1550–1500 BC. Herakleion Museum, Crete.

RIGHT: A small bathroom in the Palace of Nestor with the bath (or terracotta larnax) more or less intact. The larnax had a narrow waist shape and a convenient clay step is in front to enable the bather to get in easily. Two large jars of 1.2 metres high were found either side of the room, presumably to hold the bath water, and a kylix or wine cup was found at the bottom of the bath itself; either it was being used to pour water over the bather, or someone was drinking wine in their bath! 1300 BC. Pylos, Peloponnese, Greece.

LEFT: Fresco of a Minoan lady called by Sir
Arthur Evans, the original excavator of the
site, 'La Parisienne' because of her painted
eyes and lips and hair style. As she wears the
sacral knot at the back of her neck, she was
probably a priestess or even a goddess.
c. 1400 BC. Herakleion Museum, Crete.

ABOVE: The two figures depicted on the top
of the oenochoe (or single handled jug) are
thought to be Theseus and Ariadne. *c.* 700
BC. Herakleion Museum, Crete.

ABOVE: Two goddesses and a child carved in ivory (see p. 48); the baby is climbing from one woman to the other older one, perhaps the mother. This is typical of the young man between two women, and many such triads exist from Sumeria to Classical Greece – Adonis moving between the goddess of the underworld, Persephone, and the light of the upper world – Aphrodite. *c.*1400–1200 BC. Ref: 7711. National Archaeological Museum, Athens.

that launched a thousand ships' – and carried her off to Troy; the Greeks gathered a huge navy to rescue her. The ensuing ten-year war, thought to have been fought around 1200 BC, is the subject of Homer's great epic poem, *The Iliad*, written some four hundred years later.

The site of Troy was first discovered by an Englishman, Frank Calvert, in 1853, while he was acting as American consul in the Dardanelles. In 1863 he suggested to the British Museum that it should excavate the hill of Hissarlik, but the proposal was rejected. In the following year he himself bought the northern section of the hill and started digging, actually unearthing the remains of a temple to Athena and some traces of a Bronze Age settlement; but lack of funds forced him to stop, and it was left to the German archaeologist Heinrich Schliemann to continue the work some years later, in 1872. After three years' work Schliemann discovered what he called

'King Priam's treasure', and photographed his beautiful Greek wife Sophia (whom he had ordered, sight unseen, through the good offices of the Patriarch of Athens), wearing the jewels, which he confidently believed to have belonged to Helen herself. The jewels and other treasures – which, incidentally, are now known to predate Homeric Troy by several centuries – disappeared from the Berlin Museum during the last days of the Second World War. Only in 1996 did the Russian Ministry of Culture publicly confess that the Soviet Government had been concealing them for the past fifty years.

Homer's themes of friendship, love, sexual betrayal and revenge were a lasting inspiration to the Greeks and to the civilizations that followed them. That semi-legendary era gave way to the beginnings of recorded history, as well as to the rise of Athens and the other city-states of ancient Greece.

LEFT: Marble bust of Homer. Roman copy of lost Hellenistic 2nd-century BC original. No one knows what Homer really looked like as he died in *c.* 700 BC, but this Hellenistic blind-type interpretation is most evocative. Ref: GR 1805.7–3.85. British Museum, London.

ABOVE: Mycenaean female head, possibly a sphinx, made from lime plaster. Found near the main Grave Circle in Mycenae. *c.*1200 BC. Ref: 4575. National Archaeological Museum, Athens.

5 Gods and Men in Greece

In their way of life as in their religion, the Greeks were much influenced by the East; and one of their most significant imports, brought to them by Phoenician merchants, was the alphabet. This they refined into their own system of vowels and consonants, the basis of the alphabet that we use today. This enabled them to express complex thoughts in written words which were less awkward and ambiguous than the hieroglyphs and cuneiform writing of older civilizations; and among the first things they wrote about were the myths and legends of their gods.

Zeus, grandson of the sky-god Uranus and chief of all gods, lived with them on Mount Olympus in northern Greece. His earliest cults were thus associated with mountain tops and thunderstorms, and he is traditionally represented with a thunderbolt in each hand. He married his own sister, Hera, goddess of women and marriage; but he was consistently unfaithful to her, she was violently jealous, and the result was that the two were always quarrelling. This reflects the time when the two cults, male and female, were slowly being reconciled, the older female deity giving way to the male.

The Rise of Athens

No city could have been more male-dominated than Athens in the 5th century BC. Its principal enemy at this time was Persia, whose army the Athenians defeated at Marathon in 490 BC and whose navy they crushed at the battle of Salamis ten years later. These victories led to a dramatic rise in the city's status, which they celebrated with an ambitious building programme under the direction of their leader Pericles.

The most important of all the new buildings was the Parthenon on the Acropolis, dedicated to their tutelary goddess Pallas Athene. Begun in 447 BC and completed within ten years, it shows astonishing technical refinement. To make its proportions visually perfect, what appear to be straight lines are in fact very gentle curves. The columns not only bulge a little but actually lean imperceptibly inwards, making the building seem taller, while the platform on which they stand is very slightly convex, a few inches higher in the middle than at the edges.

At this time Athens also saw an astonishing flowering of the arts and sciences. Around 428 BC was born a man who arguably was to influence western thought more than any other: the philosopher Plato. He founded an academy of philosophy which can be seen as the world's first university, and he crystallized his thought in

OPPOSITE: In an area sacred to the goddess Hera, a section of the temple to Poseidon at Paestum (which used to be called Poseidonia) in southern Italy. *c.* 450 BC.
LEFT: The god Zeus abducting his favourite Ganymede to be his cup-bearer, as the great 'father of gods and men' had fallen in love with him. Olympia Museum, Peloponnese, Greece.
ABOVE: Bust of Plato who lived from about 429–347 BC. Roman copy of an early Greek original. Glyptothek Museum, Munich.

TOP: Athena, patron goddess of Athens, who was worshipped on the Acropolis. Patron of arts and crafts, her main role was goddess of war, as she is shown here. Athena Velletri. Ref: GL 213. Glyptothek Museum, Munich. ABOVE: Bust of Socrates. The intellectual father of Greek philosophy, whose physical appearance was famously unattractive, belying the inner beauty of his spirit. Roman copy of a 4th-century BC original. Ref: GR 1973.3–27.16. British Museum.

some thirty major philosophical works in the form of dialogues. Among these was the *Symposium*, a dinner-party conversation on the subject of love. He sets his scene on an evening in 416 BC, in the *andron* or dining room of the dramatist Agathon, who has just won a prize for his latest play; and he uses his characters to put forward a number of highly intelligent, original and occasionally even shocking views on love, as it existed for himself and his friends some 2,500 years ago. The traditional god of feasting was Dionysus, son of Zeus, and one of his many mistresses, Semele; as he was also the god of wine and associated with all expressions of emotion, any symposium worthy of the name would begin with a sacrifice to him. This was by no means the first reference to such an event. Nearly a century earlier, the poet Anacreon had mentioned symposia with wine where love was discussed.

The word *andron* means a room for men. It has been argued that the private houses of the well-to-do in ancient Greece were normally divided into two, half for men and half for women, possibly each with its separate entrance from the street so that the two sexes could come and go without disturbing each other. These symposia, held in the men's quarters, would consequently be for male guests only – though there were often slave girls to provide music and perhaps other, non-musical entertainment at a later stage. The guests might also bring their slave mistresses, or *hetairai*; or perhaps even ordinary prostitutes. To us, such a party seems a curious mixture – of eating, drinking, singing, joking and philosophical debate, all accompanied by a good deal of sexual activity. The sex, however, was never on these occasions with respectable women, only with *hetairai* or other slaves, prostitutes or boys. In short the entire household was split: on the one hand there was the domain of respectable women, and on the other that of more disreputable sexual partners. As Plato himself points out, the human soul is similarly divided: the upper department is male, the other female, secluded and of necessity inferior.

The room would be furnished with couches, set round a central table on which the food and drink would be distributed. The guests reclined on their left arm, using only their right hand to eat with. The couches were large enough for two people and could be used later for such couplings as might occur.

At Plato's symposium – the most famous of them all – the principal guest was Socrates, the stonemason's son who became celebrated as one of the greatest philosophers of the western world. He could normally be found in the *agora*, the main public square of Athens, where his young disciples would meet him for discussions.

For Socrates, nothing was sacred. He encouraged his students to question, including the role of the state and that of religion. To the authorities, not surprisingly, his views smacked of dangerous subversion and led to his death. He himself wrote nothing down; but his views were carefully recorded by his devoted follower Plato, and introduced into the dialogues.

Besides the host Agathon, there is another playwright at the symposium: the comic poet Aristophanes, whose dazzling comedies such as *The Frogs*, *The Birds* and *Lysistrata* are still performed today. Also present are Phaedrus, a slightly pedantic man of letters who chooses love as the subject of the evening's discussion; Aristodemus, whom Socrates has just met outside the baths and invited along; Pausanias, Agathon's lover and a subtle advocate of homosexual love; and Erixymachus, one of the most respected doctors practising at that time in Athens. Although Plato pokes gentle fun at his long-winded dialogue, he gives him some original ideas and comments. The last guest to arrive is Alcibiades, Pericles' adopted son, an arrogant and ambitious man who has many admirers of both sexes. His speech is about his own love for Socrates, which is not reciprocated.

BELOW: Reconstruction of the Stoa of Eumenes, which was part of the Agora where Socrates often held his listeners enthralled. Here he is walking back home, barefoot and alone in the dawn after the symposium described by Plato in 416 BC.

Symposia of this kind, and the whole leisured way of life in ancient Greece, were made possible only by the existence of huge numbers of slaves. At this time there were thought to have been about 100,000 of them – about the same number as there were free citizens.

Plato's *Symposium* begins with a speech by Phaedrus about the origins of the god of love. To the modern reader, familiar with Aphrodite, goddess of love, this may seem a little confusing; but the Greek word for love, *Eros*, is masculine, and is also the name of Aphrodite's son, the minor god of love whom the Romans were to know as Cupid. In any case, Plato's contemporaries would have immediately understood that it was really the abstract idea of love that was under discussion:

BELOW: Mosaic with the head of the god Dionysus from a Roman villa near Corinth. Dionysus was the son of Zeus and Semele and the god of wine, and so the harbinger of emotion and a cult of fertility. He was also patron god of the theatre. Ref: A609. Archaeological Museum of Corinth.

ABOVE: Aphrodite having risen from the sea sits on a shell drying her hair. She is being supported by two admiring tritons, the one on the left carries an anchor and on the right an oar. This charming interpretation of the myth of Aphrodite comes from the 'Aphrodisian school' of sculptors in the 3rd century AD. Aphrodisias, Turkey.

'That this god of love should be considered one of the most ancient of all beings certainly does him great honour: Love, as we can see, has no parents. Hesiod speaks of

>Broad-breasted Earth, on whose foundation firm
>
>Creation stands, and Love ...

while Parmenides, in speaking of Creation, says that "first among the gods she invented Love". So there is widespread agreement about the extreme antiquity of love.'

We have already seen that the earliest deities were female. According to the earliest legend of Aphrodite, quoted by Homer, she was the daughter of Zeus and his aunt Dione. Phaedrus, however, quotes from Hesiod, an early writer who, in his *Theogony*, attempted to account for the genealogy of the gods. According to him, the Earth Mother, Gaia, was made pregnant by the sky god, her brother Uranus, and produced a strange variety of offspring which included the giant Titans, one-eyed Cyclops and other monsters of various kinds. Their eldest child, Kronos, married his sister Rhea; terrified of being overthrown by his own children, he devoured his three daughters and two sons as soon as they were born. Rhea then left for the island of Crete where,

ABOVE LEFT: Aphrodite. A Roman copy of the original statue made by the great Greek sculptor Praxiteles, *c.* 350 BC, for the people of Knidos in Asia Minor. The model was the courtesan Phryne, Praxiteles' lover (see pp. 75 and 77). Glyptothek Museum, Munich. ABOVE RIGHT: Pericles, the great statesman and general (see pp. 75 and 90). He was responsible for the rebuilding of the Acropolis. Roman copy, 2nd century BC, from Tivoli. Glyptothek Museum, Munich. OPPOSITE: Temple of Aphrodite, originally completed by about 90 BC, and despite several earthquakes these Ionic columns survived. City of Aphrodisias, Turkey. Ref: GR 1805.7–3.91. British Museum.

in a cave on Mount Ida, she secretly gave birth to her next son, Zeus. Leaving the mountain nymphs to look after him, she returned home and presented Kronos with a large stone wrapped in swaddling clothes. He, assuming that this was another of his newborn children, swallowed the stone whole; but it made him so sick that he regurgitated all his other children. Still determined to secure his position as next on the throne of the gods, he prevented his father Uranus from having more children by cutting off his genitals and throwing them into the sea; and it was these that the sea spume (a sperm transmogrification) transformed into Aphrodite.

The Two Types of Love

The next speaker in the *Symposium*, Pausanias, refuses to accept the conditions laid down for the discussion, that it should be a simple panegyric of love:

'That would be perfectly acceptable if love had a single nature, but in fact it bears two distinct forms; we must therefore declare at the outset which form we wish to praise. About the first kind there can be no doubt: that is the common love that goes with

earthly Aphrodite, the love felt by men of the baser sort. This love is directed towards women just as much as it is towards young men; it is physical rather than spiritual; and it prefers its objects to be as unintelligent as possible, since its only aim is to satisfy its desires.'

This 'earthly Aphrodite' can be taken as referring to the goddess of the Homeric version, whose temple at Corinth was famous throughout the ancient world for its prostitutes. Pausanias now contrasts her with 'heavenly Aphrodite':

'The heavenly Aphrodite, goddess of spiritual love, has no female strain in her; she springs directly from the male, born as she is from the foaming brine and the severed genitals of her father Uranus whose son, to gain the throne, had cut them off and thrown them into the sea. She is consequently older, and free from all wantonness. Those who are inspired by this love are attracted to the male sex, valuing it as being both the stronger and the more intelligent.'

Pausanias' carefully-drawn distinction between the two types of Aphrodite, and thus

of love itself, leads us on to the two Greek words for love, *eros* for physical desire and *agape* for the higher, spiritual love uncontaminated by sex – the love that was later to be described as 'Platonic'. The first of these he defines as being between men and women, the second between men only, since this love is 'stronger and more intelligent'. He sums up his argument with a defence of homosexual love:

'Even among the lovers of their own sex, one can easily distinguish those who are inspired by this second love, since they do not fall in love with mere boys. Rather than running off with some fresh new darling, they wait until the object of their affection has gained intelligence and is about to grow a beard, showing that their wish is for a lasting attachment, a partnership for life.

Here in Athens things are more complex; but most cities have a moral code laid down in black and white. In Olympia and Sparta the code allows anyone of any age to take a lover; perhaps, being simple country folk, they want to avoid making long persuasive speeches to their loved ones. In Ionia, however, and in other areas under Persian rule, the laws are quite the reverse, since the Persians disapprove of such male friendships and attachments, which do not suit the interests of their government. We all know well the destabilising effect of love on the power structure of a city, since it was the passion of the Athenian tyrant Aristogeiton for Harmodius that led to his downfall.'

The reference is to a moment in Athenian history when the city was ruled by the tyrant Hippias. A Roman copy can be seen in the Naples Museum, a splendid composition of two naked warriors side by side, celebrating 'The Tyrannicides' – the two men who dared oppose the tyrant. The real motive for the murder was conveniently forgotten, male lovers of the same age being then frowned upon by Athenian society.

Friendships, on the other hand, between a man in his twenties and a pubescent boy were given warm approval, being supposed to have an educational value. The *erastes,* or lover, would instruct the young boy – his *eromenos,* or beloved – in the arts and the ways of society. In her book *The Reign of the Phallus*, Professor Eva Keuls has discussed these relationships at length:

'The idealized pattern of behaviour to which Plato refers among others, is the relationship between a mature man and a young boy which was consummated intercrurally, meaning between the thighs. In other words, the young partner faced his older lover and there was a certain feeling of reciprocity involved, which is made clear from evidence in vase paintings. The consummation by anal sex at all ages was greatly frowned upon and is widely derided by Aristophanes himself in several of his comedies. In fact the playwright Agathon, the host at the symposium, is the frequent butt of Aristophanes' jokes because Agathon evidently continued pederastic practices beyond the canonical age. He also had a tendency towards adopting effeminate poses, which on the whole was not part of the Greek homosexual idea, and Aristophanes makes brutal fun of Agathon in his plays, but not in the symposium.'

OPPOSITE ABOVE: Aphrodite with Pan and her son Eros. Aphrodite has raised her sandal to ward off the sexual advances of Pan, while Eros joins in to help his mother. 1st century AD from the island of Delos. Height 1.30 metres. Ref: 3335. National Archaeological Museum, Athens.

OPPOSITE BELOW: Another aspect of the Temple of Aphrodite's columns. 90 BC City of Aphrodisias, Turkey.

ABOVE: Harmodius and Aristogiton killed Hipparchus, brother of the ruling tyrant Hippias in 514 BC. Harmodius was the lover of Aristogiton. He had rejected advances from Hipparchus who, furious at being spurned, accused Harmodius of being an effeminate debauchee and prevented his sister from carrying a basket in a procession up the Acropolis. The quarrel became so intense that the two lovers used the procession as a moment to murder Hipparchus. However the guards killed Harmodius instantly and Aristogiton died later under prolonged torture. Naples Museum, Italy.

As for Agathon and Pausanias, they seem to have stayed together for most of their adult lives. At the time of the *Symposium*, Agathon would have been about thirty. When he left Athens nine years later in 407 BC, Pausanias went with him. Plato makes Aristophanes much gentler towards Agathon in his play *The Wasps* – in which he pokes fun at what he calls 'the gentlemen's intellectual symposium' – even giving him a speech in which he holds up the relationship as an fine example of stability:

'So whenever someone has the good fortune to encounter his own actual other half, affection, kinship and love combine in an emotion so overwhelming that such a pair practically refuse ever to be separated, even for a moment. No one therefore can suppose it is mere physical enjoyment which causes the one to take such intense delight in the company of the other.'

Aristophanes raises his drinking cup.

'So let no man set himself in opposition to Love, for if we are his friends we shall succeed in finding the person to love who in the strictest sense belongs to us. I know that Eryximachus is anxious to make fun of my speech, but he is not supposed to

BELOW: The interior of a Greek tomb, and how the 'Tomb of the Diver' would have been assembled. In this tomb, Nike or Victory (representing the triumphant survival of death to an afterlife) rides her chariot between the setting and rising suns. The pomegranates, which can just be seen hanging on the left, are a symbol of life after death. Made in Paestum in about 325 BC. Tomba no. 86. Paestum Museum, Italy.

think I am pointing to Pausanias and Agathon. They are unquestionably two halves at last united, but I am speaking of men and women in general when I say the way to happiness for our race lies in fulfilling the behests of Love.'

The Tomb of the Diver and a Colonial Symposium

By the time that Plato was writing his *Symposium* in in Athens, the city's influence had spread as far as the Greek colonies of Magna Graecia in southern Italy. The ancient city of Paestum near Salerno is justly famous for its magnificent Greek temples; less well known is its Museum, in which we can see several illustrations of sexual behaviour at gatherings of the kind Plato described. Paestum was greatly influenced by Sybaris, on the south coast in the Gulf of Tavanto about 100 miles away, whose inhabitants, the Sybarites, were so dedicated to luxury and pleasure that

ABOVE: Part of the 'Tomb of the Diver'. The man with the stick is probably the master of ceremonies, who enters with the young man (ephebe), carrying a small blue chitoniskos, and the flute-girl (the only woman present) dressed in white. 475 BC. Paestum Museum, Italy.

65

they have given a word – 'sybaritic' – to the language. In Paestum archaeologists recently uncovered the only known Greek painted tomb of this period – the so-called 'Tomb of the Diver' – which certainly reinforces the city's sybaritic behaviour.

Painted on the walls of small tomb is a detailed scene of a symposium. The guests, all men, are reclining on couches, sometimes singly, sometimes in pairs. One guest offers a kylix of wine to a young man in a blue *chitoniskos*, who is about to join the party. He is led in by a female flute player – the only girl present. There has already been a good deal of drinking. Now the first musicians have laid down their lyres and it is the turn of the flutes, whose music seems to entrance one of the guests. The bearded older man's half-open mouth, staring eyes and gesture towards his red-lipped young companion reveal his feelings all too clearly, despite the boy's protests. The two are watched by another guest, who seems mildly surprised by what is going on, while his companion raises his kylix to throw the last drops of wine. This game was called kottabos; if the wine drops hit the target, the thrower won the object of his desire.

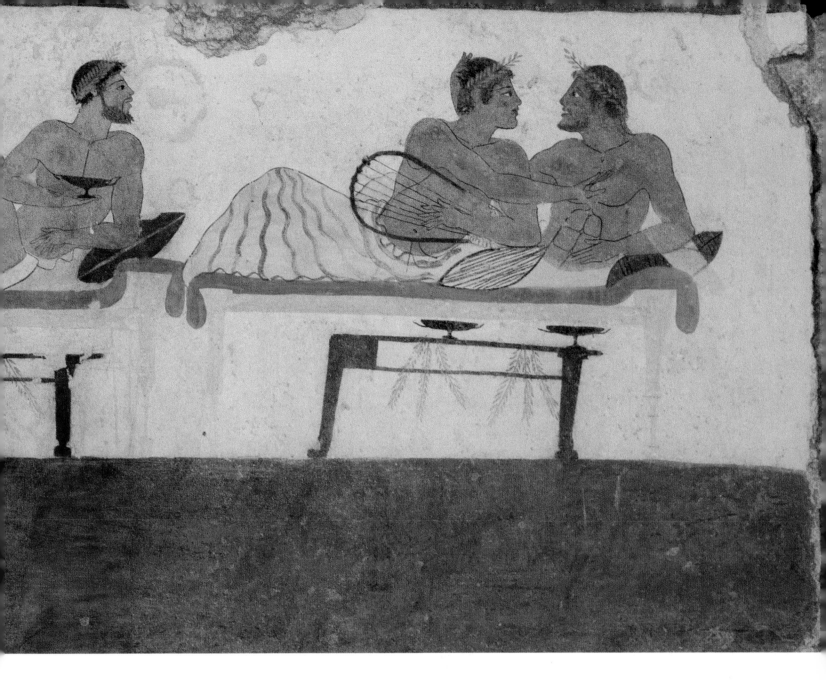

On the lid of the tomb (on loan to Venice when we visited), a naked man is diving into the sea. Does this simply illustrate the deceased's love of swimming, or is it a symbolic representation of his soul entering the unknown depths of the afterlife? We cannot be sure – although the charmingly painted diving board and the blue and welcoming sea seem a long way from the sinister river Styx and the ferry of Charon.

Sparta, Sex and Sport

Among the independent Greek city-states, attitudes to homosexuality differed from one to the next. In the warlike city-states such as Sparta, homosexuality was accepted. Plato reports that young boys were taken away from their mothers at the age of seven and were sent to military barracks in Sparta where they lived, ate and slept with their elders. Moreover, on the night of a Spartan wedding, the bride had to lie in a dark room wearing a man's cloak and sandals, waiting for her husband – a ritual of transition, perhaps, to help take the husband from his all-male world to the

ABOVE: The 'Tomb of the Diver'. The frescoed tomb walls were painted by the artist in his workshop on to damp plaster and then lowered into place in situ. The calcium carbonate of the lime plaster compound and the carbon dioxide formed a hard crystalline surface as the plaster slowly dried, so protecting the painting for two and a half thousand years. *c*. 475 BC. Paestum Museum, Italy.

ABOVE: Pyramidal stele with reliefs representing Helen of Troy and Menelaus or Agamemnon and Clytemnestra. Archaic period. Sparta Museum, Peloponnese, Greece.

world of the heterosexual. Even when Spartan men were married they still lived in barracks, and could only surreptitiously sneak out at night to visit their wives.

In another city, Thebes, we know that homosexuality in the armed forces was actively encouraged. In the *Symposium* Plato mentions lovers being paired up in the army, probably referring to the Spartans:

'Yet there is a difference between the lover and the beloved, since the latter is peculiarly sensitive to dishonour in the presence of his lover. One could not contrive a better fighting force than a handful of such men fighting side by side. A lover would rather die than be seen by his beloved to be deserting his post. Moreover, only lovers will sacrifice their lives for each other. This is true of women as well as men.'

Twenty years after the *Symposium* was written, the Theban general Epaminondas organized a regiment of three hundred men consisting of 150 pairs of lovers. The famous 'Band of Thebes' constituted a formidable fighting force, with lover defending lover to the death. They were finally beaten by King Philip of Macedon – father of Alexander the Great – at the battle of Chaeronea in 338 BC. When Philip saw the slaughtered regiment, with all the fallen soldiers lying in pairs and their mortal wounds at the front, and was told that they were all each other's lovers, he wept. 'Accursed be those,' he murmured, 'who could ever imagine that such heroes could ever be guilty of a deed of shame.'

The association between war and athletics goes as far back as 800 BC: Homer describes a King referring to his son as 'the fastest runner and a warrior'. In the great years of Sparta its youth, both boys and girls, trained naked, and it is thought that these tough Peloponnesians were also responsible for the introduction of nakedness into the Olympic games. (Another explanation was that during one of the early contests the athlete Osyppus of Megara lost his loincloth in the middle of a race, and with his new-found freedom streaked to victory.)

In all ancient Greek sports nudity was the rule for men; and Plutarch, writing many years after Plato, blamed this practice for the spread of pederasty. Every young man was expected both to train and to study in his local gymnasium: the word *gymnos* actually means 'naked'. The manager was known as a gymnasiarch, and there was also a trainer to ensure fair play. For the all-round contestant, the main event was the pentathlon, or combination of five events: throwing the discus and javelin, running, jumping and wrestling. In 628 BC a boys' pentathlon was introduced to the Olympic Games, and was won by a Spartan. It was immediately discontinued, perhaps because it was

ABOVE: A votive relief dedicated to the two sons of Zeus called the 'Dioscuri' by Kallicrates, emphasizing the Spartan treatment of the athletic body in repose. Sparta Museum, Greece.

considered too much of a strain on the athletes; alternatively, the winner may have been thought to have enjoyed an unfair advantage.

Before the games the contestants covered their bodies in oil, and then sprinkled them with sand to prevent sunburn. Later they would scrape themselves clean with a special instrument known as a strigil.

The physical appearance of the pentathlete was admired by the Greeks for its overall balance and proportions. Excessive musculature was frowned on, as – according to Aristophanes – was over-development of the genitals:

'In those days [i.e. when he was young] not one of the lads ever rubbed himself with oil below the navel, but left a down-like covering on his lower body, so as not to incite lustful glances. The gymnastic trainer compelled the boys to stretch out their legs when they sat down, in order to prevent any shocking exposure to the spectators. When they stood up they were obliged to smooth down the sand on which they had sat, lest they leave any imprint of their masculinity to meet the eyes of lovers.'

Women and the Games

Women did not participate in the Olympics but had their own, smaller, religious games dedicated to the goddess Hera, earlier in the year. Here these games are described by the Greek historian Pausanias:

'The games consist of a running contest between sixteen virgin girls; they run with their hair let down and their tunics above their knees, with the right breast and shoulder bared. The winners receive crowns of olive branches and a share of the ox which is sacrificed to Hera.'

Portraits of the winners were hung in the Temple of Hera; but these were paintings, not sculptures, so no statues survive. There is, however, a bronze statuette of a woman athlete, her costume just as Pausanias describes it. The girls' trainers were often their mothers – occasionally with some strange results. Professor Theo Antikas explains:

'There was a famous mother from the island of Rhodes by the name of Pherenike, which in Greek means "bringer of victory". Other historians however prefer to call her Kallipatera, which means "of a good father", because her father was an Olympic winner. So were her brothers. Pherenike had a son, and as his father had died she decided that she would train him in boxing herself. The son was an excellent young athlete, and Pherenike was determined that he should win the boxing event. She therefore dressed herself as a male trainer, thus breaking the law that forbade women to enter the area of the Games.

Having got herself secretly into the trainers' stands, she sat behind a fence ... and watched excitedly as her son won his first bout and then took on the finalist. To her great joy her boy won, continuing the family tradition. When he was declared the victor, such was her excitement that she jumped for joy; but her male clothing tore on the wooden fence, and as she fell everyone saw that she was a woman.

According to Pausanias this was a crime; but it put the extremely strict Olympic judges – the Ellanodikai – in a quandary. Here was a woman whose father, brothers and son were all Olympic winners; they could hardly sentence her, as the rules required, to a public flogging. They eventually forgave her; but they also passed a law according to which, in the future Olympics, not only the athletes had to be naked but trainers as well.'

OPPOSITE ABOVE: Two athletes in the gymnasium, one massaging the back of his companion before wrestling. Note hanging on the wall on the left the oil bottle and scraper (strigil) to get the sand and mud off the body after leaving the palaestra or wrestling area. Athenian red-figured cup. 420 BC. Ref: 5043. Villa Giulia Museum, Italy.

OPPOSITE BELOW: Bearded older man making sexual approaches to a younger man in the gymnasium. Black-figure Attic skyphos. c. 560 BC. Ref: 2067. Tarquinia Museum, Italy.

BELOW: Two young uninhibited boys examining the interior of a bowl. Ref: 697. Tarquinia Museum, Italy.

There was only one exception to the rule banning women from the Olympic Games: the High Priestess of Demeter, the corn goddess who was linked with fertility and the regenerative powers of the earth. She had a special seat next to the statue of the goddess, half-way along the stadium and opposite the stand of the Ellanodikai themselves. Was this privilege accorded her by reason of some ancient ritual celebrating the first and oldest female divinity, Gaia, or Mother Earth herself? It seems possible, but we shall never know.

Self-love and the Story of Narcissus

Modern psychologists believe that homosexual love is often linked to the love of oneself, or narcissism. This word is derived from the Greek fable of Narcissus, son of the river god Cephisus. Such was his beauty that everyone fell in love with him, but their love was never returned. One day he was out hunting with some friends; he thought he heard a stag in the nearby woods and set off by himself to investigate. The sound in fact came from the nymph Echo, who was in love with him and hiding in a tree. After searching for a while in vain, he reached a waterfall and, suddenly realizing he was lost, began calling to his friends: 'Where are you?' To his surprise, the question came back to him: 'Where are you?' 'I'm here,' he answered; 'I'm here,' came the reply. At last he found Echo in her tree, but as always he spurned her love. 'I will die,' he told her, 'before you ever lie with me', and turned to leave. Once again his words came back to him: 'Lie with me!' – but he had already gone, leaving Echo sad and alone.

ABOVE: Bronze female figurine as a mirror handle; as she is wearing a diazoma or shorts, she could be an athlete. Found on the Greek island of Aegina. Ref: 7703. National Archaeological Museum, Athens.

RIGHT: Narcissus by the pool. This was painted in 1640 by Van Keijl, and sums up the Renaissance romanticism of ancient Greek myths. Ref: SN885. John and Mable Ringling Museum of Art, USA.

LEFT: Man with young boy. They are at the gymnasium as the strigil or scraper (see p. 71), and a sponge, can be seen hanging on the wall. This is a copy by Alpha Arts of an original Greek *kylix*.

BELOW: Female figurine from Sparta, probably an athlete. Ref: 15897. National Archaeological Museum, Athens.

Narcissus stopped by a spring to quench his thirst, caught sight of his own reflection and immediately fell in love with it. He tried to embrace the image, but found that it was impossible. How could he endure this anguish of possessing and yet not possessing? Some say he died of a broken heart, others that he stabbed himself to death and that from the drops of blood that fell to the earth there sprang up the red-centred flower that we still call by his name. Poor Echo – whose heart was certainly broken – spent the rest of her life pining for him and wasting away in the lonely hills of Arcadia, until only her voice remained. It is a simple enough fable, about the vanity of man; but it has inspired poets and painters for the better part of three thousand years.

Homosexuality and the Law of Athens

Despite the seemingly tolerant attitude to sex among the leisured classes of Athenian society, boys enjoyed a certain amount of protection from Athenian law. Aeschines gives us a revealing insight into the Athenian view of prostitution, whether male or female:

'If a father, brother, uncle or tutor sells a boy to a man of licentious character the child will not be prosecuted, but the other parties will be. For the Law of Outrage decrees that the assailant of a child, whether the victim be free or a slave, shall be

RIGHT: Older boy making advances to a younger one, who is protesting, in the gymnasium. Kylix or drinking cup. Ref: 698. Tarquinia Museum, Italy.

BELOW: Man having sex with a prostitute from behind. Drinking cup by the Briseis Painter. Ref: 2984. Tarquinia Museum, Italy.

charged and the due penalty applied, or else he shall pay a fine determined by the court. Any Athenian who prostitutes himself shall be charged with hetairesis – lack of principle – an offence punishable with the utmost rigour of the law.'

The word *hetairesis,* clearly linked with the word *hetaira,* could be translated as 'harlotry'. But let us now look rather more closely at the hetairai themselves.

Hetairai, *Courtesans and Prostitutes*

Our most important source of knowledge of these ladies is Greek vase painting. On one vase an older man is shown holding up his purse, ready to purchase the favours of some boys. His travel bag is hanging on the wall – a sure sign that he's from out of town. Another purse is also being offered by a client to a hetaira.

In another image, hetairai cavort with their legs in the air and with their wine cups raised. The most celebrated of these high-class courtesans – many of whom became rich and famous – was Aspasia, mistress of the great general Pericles. Despite the fact that, coming as she did from the city of Miletus in Asia Minor, she could never aspire to become accepted as Athenian, Pericles – who was himself Governor of Athens at the time – divorced his wife and took Aspasia to live with him as his concubine. Socrates rated her intelligence very highly, and she held amusing and fascinating salons; nevertheless, Athenian society was deeply shocked by this beautiful and charming Milesian lady who stayed with Pericles – they were obviously very much in love – until he died of the plague in 429 BC.

Another famous hetaira – who lived a century after Aspasia – was Phryne. She too became enormously rich. One of her lovers was the great sculptor Praxiteles, to whom she gave the inspiration for his statues of Aphrodite. On one occasion she was charged with profane behaviour and put on trial; defending her was another of her lovers, the orator Hyperides. Seeing that he was making no progress in the case he suddenly decided to take a completely different line of defence: he tore down her dress, revealing a pair of perfect breasts. Confronted by such beauty, the judges could only acquit her – though a new law was passed immediately afterwards, forbidding the accused to be present in court while the verdict was under consideration.

BELOW: Man having anal sex with prostitute. A pelike jug. Ref: RC 2989. Tarquinia Museum, Italy.

Praxiteles's most famous statue of Phryne was the Aphrodite of Knidos (see p. 60) – sometimes known, in its Latin form, as the Cnidian Venus. The original is lost, like all the sculptor's works except one (the marble statue of Hermes with the infant Dionysus, found at Olympia, see p. 84); but there is a good Roman copy of this work in the Munich Glyptothek. The subject was originally naked; but the people of the island of Kos for whom it was originally intended were shocked by the nudity and demanded a draped version, so the people of Knidos bought the other. The statue was famous throughout the ancient world, not only as a *succès de scandale* but for its astonishing beauty. Like most ancient statues, it was originally coloured, the painters sometimes being paid even more than the sculptors themselves. The Knidans built their Aphrodite a special temple, with an entrance at the back as well as the front, since she was equally beautiful from all angles. There were even stories of people falling in love with her; one young man was reputed to have slipped into the temple at night and left all too obvious proof of his love-making to be discovered in the morning – though stories like this may have been deliberately propagated by the Knidans in order to encourage visitors to their shrine.

The prosperous port of Corinth also had a famous temple of Aphrodite, where the most beautiful and sought-after prostitutes plied their trade. In 464 BC a Corinthian athlete named Xenophon promised the goddess a hundred girls if he

OPPOSITE: Group sex painted on a 'Tyrrhenian' amphora. Ref: 1432. Antikensammlung, Munich.
BELOW: Men behaving badly, and in a drunken dance, they make their way to a symposium. The party which came with Alcibiades to Plato's symposium were behaving in this manner. Drinking cup. Ref: 50396. Villa Giulia Museum, Rome.

ABOVE: Interior of previous drinking cup (see illustration on p. 77) which appears to be a woman dressed as a man in perhaps some Dionysian transvestite revelry. Professor Eva Keuls thinks that it shows a woman wearing a false beard taking part in the 'Skira' ritual, where roles were changed and the women organized their own mock parliament. Ref: 50396, Villa Giulia Museum, Rome.

won the Olympic games that year. He did so, and paid his debt – to the satisfaction, no doubt, of not only Aphrodite herself but of many sailors and travellers as well. In another major port, Ephesus, the girls wore sandals with reversed lettering on the sole, so that they stamped 'follow me' on the sand as they walked. A carved stone footprint of a similar kind can still be seen on a paving-stone in the city ruins.

The girls shown in the illustration (on p. 79) dancing round a phallus are probably *hetairai*; but similar dances still continue to this day – survivals from the ancient rites of spring. In most the explicit phallus has been replaced by a maypole; but in Bourani, a small town in northern Greece, a festival featuring both maypoles and phalluses is held every year. The men still wear large phalluses under their clothing, producing them at appropriate moments to tease the women. Pottery drinking vessels are made in the same shape.

The Third Sex

In the *Symposium*, Plato gives the comic playwright Aristophanes an amusing speech on the subject of love, written in a pastiche of the writer's own style. Aristophanes tells his listeners the story of Hermaphrodite, who combined the beauty of his divine parents, Hermes and Aphrodite. In the usual version of the story, Hermaphroditus was loved by the nymph Salmacis, who inhabited a fountain in which he used to bathe. He cared nothing for her, but she embraced him and prayed that their bodies would fuse together. Her wish was granted, and the two became a single being in which both sexes were combined. Aristophanes, however, produces a slightly different version:

LEFT: A naked and clothed girl are dancing around a large phallus, a reminder of the ancient dance where the maypole remains a symbol of the phallus and the coming of spring and new fertility. There is still a phallic festival with a maypole dance in northern Greece today at Bourani. Ref: 50404. Villa Giulia Museum, Rome.

ABOVE: Terracotta ithyphallic figure, possibly representing an earth cult. 6th century BC. Found in Boetia. Height 11 cms. Ref: 938. National Archaeological Museum, Athens.

'I shall try and initiate you into the secrets of love. First of all you must learn of the changes undergone by the human race. In the beginning there existed not two sexes as there are now, but three. The third, which was both male and female, has vanished; only its name still remains – the hermaphrodite, a distinct sex in form as well as in name, with characteristics of both male and female.'

The famous Sleeping Hermaphrodite in the Louvre shows all the ambiguous beauty of the third sex.

Speaking through the character of Aristophanes, Plato uses the dual sexuality of Hermaphroditus to explain his theory of the origin of the sexes – and a very curious theory it is. According to him, all the three original sexes – male, female and hermaphrodite – had two heads and four legs, and moved about by doing cart-wheels. Gradually, however, they became arrogant, to the point at which they attacked the gods. Whereupon Zeus, in revenge, divided them all into two, and moved their sexual organs to the front:

OPPOSITE: Man lifting a woman's dress done with some humour. The cock on the left of the painting was a standard homosexual love-gift. OnePossibly this was a wine jug made for someone who would understand the joke about his friend's curiosity. Ref: 2989. Tarquinia Museum, Italy.

ABOVE: Hermaphrodite asleep on a couch. The sculpture is a Roman copy of a lost Greek original, and the squared cushion mattress was added by the Italian scultor Giovanni Lorenzo Bernini in the 1620s, who seems to have added other things as well! 2nd century BC. Length 1.50 meters. Ref: Ma 231. Louvre Museum, Paris.

81

BELOW: The *hetaira* on this large symposium cup-skyphos is offering a symposium drinking cup to a mule with an erection. Stories of this coarse nature later formed part of the novel *The Golden Ass* by Lucius Apuleius, a young Roman who travelled widely in Greece in 125 AD. His theme is of a man turned into an ass and of his adventures in Greece. Cup-skyphos by Epiktetos from Anzi *c.* 5th century BC. Ref: RP 27669. Archaeological Museum, Naples. OPPOSITE: Two naked *hetairai*, probably at their toilette. However this drinking cup by Apollodorus was painted by a man for men at a symposium, all of whom knew that the pictographic short-hand to show male homosexuality was done by painting one man touching the other's genital area. So it could be assumed the same counted for women as seen by men. Kylix by Apollodorus 5th century BC. Tarquinia Museum, Italy.

'We are each of us therefore in search of our other half. So those men who are halves of the third sex, which as I told you was called hermaphrodite, are lovers of women, while those women of similar origins are lovers of men; for all of them are for ever searching for their other half. Meanwhile women who are halves of the female sex, and men who are halves of the male, direct their attentions to the same sex and are homosexual.'

And so, ever since Zeus divided the three original sexes into two, man has been eternally seeking his lost other half. When he finds it, it is love at first sight.

'Where Burning Sappho Loved and Sung'

Female homosexuality is called lesbianism after the island of Lesbos (now Mitylene), since this island was the home of Sappho – the one famous female poet of the ancient world, who made no secret of her own homosexual proclivities.

Hardly any surviving Greek paintings show scenes of lesbianism, although there is a vase painting of two *hetairai* washing together which could have sexual undertones, since one of them is touching the genitals of the other. In the many vase paintings of men such a gesture is an obvious sign of love.

Sappho was born some time in seventh century BC. She probably trained young girls in the art of singing and the dance for the many festivals which were held on

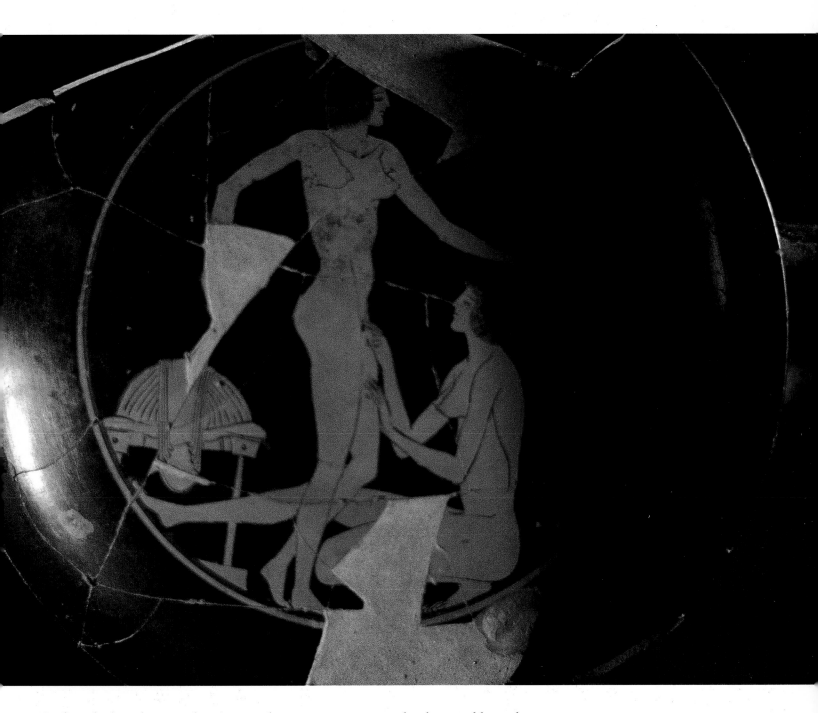

Lesbos during the year; her intense love poems were nearly always addressed to young women. She was famous in her lifetime, and her work – which was passionate, simple and direct, and completely different from that of contemporary male poets – would certainly have been well known to Plato. Unfortunately only two complete odes of hers survive. Of her other poems only small fragments of these have been found, mainly in waste tips of Egyptian papyrus, where they have been preserved by the dryness of the desert – a clear indication of how far her fame and influence had spread:

I taught her well –
      that Hero:
quick-sprinting girl
      from Gyara.

The eroticism and torment in her poem on falling in love remain unsurpassed:

Your magical laughter – this I swear –
Batters my heart – my breast astir.
My voice when I see you suddenly near
      Refuses to come.

My tongue breaks up and a delicate fire
Runs through my flesh; I see not a thing
With my eyes, and all that I hear
      In my ears is a hum.

ABOVE: Hermes holding the child Dionysus in his arms. This is the only sculpture to have come down to us by Praxiteles. As well as being the son of Zeus and Maia, he was the father of Hermaphrodite with Aphrodite (see p. 81) and invented the lyre by stringing cow-gut across a tortoiseshell which he presented to Apollo (see p. 99). 4th century BC. Museum at Olympia.

RIGHT: Woman with two dildos (*olisboi* in Greek, which were usually made of leather) and a basin. Again another male fantasy at the bottom of a symposium drinking cup, however the fragment from a cup in St Petersburg by Epiktetos has been copied in this instance on to a small jug by Alpha Arts.

The juices run down, a shuddering takes
Me in every part, and pale as the drying
Grasses, then, I think I am near
The moment of dying.

Sappho had a daughter called Cleïs.

Once I saw a very gentle
little girl picking flowers.

It gives me joy to think
I have a pretty little girl
lovely as a golden flower;
Cleïs, whom I so adore
I would not take all Lydia
Nor Lesbos (even lovelier)
in exchange for her.

ABOVE: A possible head of Sappho, or Aphrodite. Roman copy. Ref: T246. Archaeological Museum, Corinth.

Sappho is thought to have been a small, dark, unimpressive woman; but Socrates called her 'the beautiful Sappho' because of her songs.

Socrates and Love

Socrates' own views on love are expressed in the *Symposium*, unusually, through the voice of a woman, Diotima from Mantinea, who may or may not be fictitious.

'The purpose of love is to procreate and bring forth in beauty,' she said.

'But why should the object of love be procreation,' I [Socrates] asked.

'Because procreation is the nearest attainable thing to immortality, and the argument leads us to the inevitable conclusion that love is love of immortality, as well as simply of what is good. The only way in which this immortality can be achieved is by procreation, which secures the continual replacement of an old member of the race by a new.'

Later on in the evening Alcibiades – a handsome but obstreperous young man – gatecrashes the party with a group of noisy friends. The adopted son of Pericles, he was close to the source of power in Athens and consequently treated with some deference. This is what he had to say about his love for Socrates:

'Believing that he was serious in his admiration of my charms I invited him to dine with me, behaving just like a lover who has designs on his favourite. He was in no hurry to accept my invitation, but at last he agreed to come. Immediately after dinner he rose to take his leave, but I obliged him to stay, on the grounds that it was now too late for him return home. So he settled down once more on the couch on which he had reclined at dinner, next to my own. There was nobody sleeping in the room but ourselves.

When the lights were extinguished and the servants had withdrawn, I decided to come straight to the point. I told him that he was the only lover that I had had who was worthy of me, but that I suspected that he was afraid to confess his passion. I added that my ambition was to come as near perfection as possible, and that no one could give me such valuable assistance towards this object.'

'My dear Alcibiades,' Socrates replied, 'if what you say about me is true, and I really do have the power to help you improve yourself, you must be a very sharp fellow. You must also see in me a beauty which is incomparably superior to your own outstanding good looks; and if, having made this discovery, you are trying to exchange your beauty for mine, you obviously mean to get much the better of the bargain, for you are trying to get true beauty in return for sham.'

Alcibiades, not in the least put out by this response, then tries to seduce Socrates by putting his cloak and arm around him; but Socrates, ignoring his advances, takes no notice and goes to sleep.

'As it was winter, I got up and covered him with my own clothes. Then I lay down under his own worn cloak and threw my arms round this truly superhuman being and remained thus the whole night long. But I swear by all the gods that, for anything that happened between us, I might have been sleeping with my father or elder brother.'

The *Symposium* gives us only a sketchy idea of the views of Plato and his friends on the question of women and love. There is, however, a little more to be found in another of his dialogues, the *Republic*: his blueprint for an ideal society, in which he proposed equal education for both men and women. This went completely against the accepted Greek view. Aristotle, who was a pupil of Plato's at the Academy, thought that woman was in a way incomplete – a sort of unfinished man. There was therefore, he believed, no point in educating her; education would not even affect her children, since all the inherited characteristics of the child came from the sperm of the male. Aristotle's view of love was equally uncompromising: he believed that all nature was based on cause and effect – in other words, that one person would love another only for what he or she could gain from the relationship.

Here, then, are two radically different male views, in a male-dominated society. How did such a attitudes actually affect women's lives?

6 *Women in Athens*

Few people know more about women's life in ancient Greece than Dr Ellen Reeder.
At a recent exhibition on Women in Classical Greece, which was mounted for the
Walters Art Gallery in Munich, she spoke about love and marriage from the point of
view of the bride:

'Well, it's certainly true that her marriage was arranged. It's also certainly true that at
14 she would be married to a man whom she may never have met or may have
known only vaguely. Still, given that, I think that a bride went into marriage with a
great deal of hope and expectation. Remember that she had been raised for this
moment. At this moment she thought that she was the most beautiful, desirable
woman there could be.

She had been told by society that she was at the height of her womanly powers
and charm. That she was sexy, that she was desirable for her fertility, for her dowry, for
her textile-making skills. I think she really had been convinced that it would be
impossible for a man not to fall in love with her at this moment.

I think that a married woman would have known that the young female slave
might well have been having sex with her husband. However, despite the attitude to
women there was a great deal of sex between husbands and wives; we know that
because of Aristophanes. The premise of the whole of his amusing play Lysistrata is
that women will be able to make an anti-war statement by withholding sex from
their husbands. The scheme turns out to be very successful. The men are really quite
aghast, quite in agony, that they are not able to have sex with their wives.'

Women, Love and War

Love and sex certainly constitute one of the main themes in *Lysistrata*; the other is
the protracted war between Athens and Sparta, which by 412 BC, when Aristophanes

RIGHT: *Lysistrata* by Aristophanes. Lysistrata persuades the other women present to swear an oath that they will refrain from having sex with their husbands or boyfriends until Athenians and Spartans stop fighting their interminable war. This extract from the play was performed for the film "Love in the Ancient World" in Athens by (from left to right) Constantina Varsami, Alexandra Pavlidou, Antigone Amanitou as Lysistrata and Maria Panourgia, under the direction of Christopher Miles.

ABOVE: Terracotta model of a Greek woman grinding corn. 450 BC from the island of Rhodes. British Museum.

wrote his comedy, had been going on for twenty years – with only a short-lived peace after a lucky Athenian victory at the island of Sphacteria in the Peloponnese. In the play, the women of both Athens and Sparta resolve to refuse all sex with their menfolk until they stop fighting. The play – which is frequently hilarious – is still performed today, its message about the futility of war as valid now as it was 2,500 years ago.

The idea of Greek women rebelling was probably even funnier to the ancient Greeks. The ideal Greek woman in those days was supposed to be obedient and docile, spending most of her life at home, in the service of her husband and children. The only place that they would normally meet would be at the local fountain, so this is where Lysistrata hatches her plot, persuading all the women of Athens to keep away from their husbands and lovers and, among other things, never to allow their slippers to point towards the ceiling. When they have all repeated the oath, a woman called Lampito is despatched down to Sparta to spread the word there. Lysistrata and the others rush up to the Acropolis, which the older women of Athens have already captured.

After a while the lack of sexual gratification begins to have a dreadful effect on the Athenian and Spartan men alike. In ancient Greek comedies the actors wore large phalluses, which would have been hoisted to represent huge, aching erections. Also stiffened is their resolve to begin negotiations immediately, and Sparta sends a commission to Athens for this purpose. At the end of the play a treaty is signed: Lysistrata has won the day (see illustration, p. 91).

Adonis and the Festival for Women

Another of the few occasions when Greek women could get together outside their own houses was during the festival of Adonis. It was held to mourn the death of the beautiful young favourite of Aphrodite: and every spring there could be heard, from every rooftop in the city, the frenzied wailing of the women of Athens.

The legend of Adonis had its origins in Syria, whence it came via Cyprus to Greece. Adonai means 'Lord' in Hebrew, and similar words exist in other Semitic languages. In the original myth, Adonis was the lover of the earth-goddess Innana-Ishtar; according to the Greek legend, however, he was born in Paphos of an incestuous relationship between Cinyras, King of Cyprus, and his daughter Myrrha. She was allegedly in love with her father and one night, with the help of her nurse, tricked him into sleeping with her. When Cinyras found out, he was mad with rage; Myrrha fled from him terrified, and pleaded with Zeus for protection. He turned her into a myrrh tree, which ten months later split open to reveal the baby Adonis.

LEFT: Two men wearing himations – the younger one is looking down, surprised at the other's erection. This echoes the theme in Aristophanes' play *Lysistrata* when the Spartans come to Athens to complain about the women's anti-sexual behaviour, only to discover that both sides are supporting agonizing erections. On the stage this would have been portrayed in a less subtle manner! Inf no 692. Tarquinia Museum, Italy.

ABOVE: A symposium scene with *hetairai* (prostitutes) on the underneath of a *kylix* (drinking cup). The girl on the right holds up her *kylix* as if she is about to play *kottabos*, an after-dinner game in which the player has to hit their beloved with the last drops of wine in their cup. She leans on the naked leg of the man on her left, whose *chiton* has been pulled down, exposing his genitals. The girl on the extreme right is showing the man on her left that her wine cup is empty. *c.* 470–460 BC. By the Tarquinia Painter. Antikenmuseum, Basel, Switzerland.

Aphrodite was so captivated by this beautiful child that she hid him in a chest, which she entrusted for safekeeping to Persephone, Queen of the Underworld; but Persephone broke her promise and opened the chest. On seeing Adonis, she too immediately fell in love with him and refused to give him back. Aphrodite, furious, appealed to Zeus, who ruled that Adonis should spend half the year with Persephone and half with Aphrodite; but Ares, god of war and Aphrodite's lover, was consumed by jealousy. One day, when Adonis was out hunting in the forests beneath Mount Idalion, he disguised himself as a wild boar, gored Adonis in the thigh and killed him; whereupon the distraught Aphrodite turned the drops of his blood that had fallen on the ground into a scarlet flower, the anemone. Even today, anemones are still called 'the blood of Adonis' when, like Adonis on his annual journey from the Underworld, they emerge in early spring.

In their mourning ceremonies, the women would plant quick-growing seeds, like lettuce and fennel, in shallow earth contained in pieces of broken pottery. The seedlings were deliberately given only a minimum of water, so they should quickly spring up and then die prematurely, just as Adonis did, in the summer heat. Then, like Aphrodite, the women would lament his untimely return to the Underworld.

In a vase from Dr Reeder's exhibition, 'Pandora', a woman can be seen climbing a ladder to her rooftop (see p. 93), while Eros hands her the broken vessel containing the seedlings. The other half of the pot lies on the floor next to an urn of incense, composed principally of myrrh in honour of Adonis' mother Myrrha. Dr Reeder also points out that the festival represents another form of woman's rebellion, since the deliberate allowing of the seeds to die is the exact opposite of what is expected of them as mothers. They are also lamenting the death of a youth who never attained manhood, who never had a son, and who all too clearly lacked hunting skills – the precise reverse of the ideal of the Greek male.

Even today, in certain villages in Greek Macedonia, on the Friday nine days before Easter the women prepare shallow clay plates with seedlings in them. One of them, when asked what she was doing, replied, 'Oh, it's time for the Adonis'. But neither she nor any of her friends had any idea of the origin of the custom.

Woman as Vessel

The importance of the broken pots in which the seedlings were planted was that

LEFT: The bearded man is about to beat the *hetaira* he is gripping by the ankle, while the other man protests. A copy of a cup by the Antiphon Painter by Alpha Arts.

ABOVE: On this tiny squat *lekythos* container a woman is climbing a ladder to go to her roof-top for the Adonai festival. Eros is handing her a broken vessel in which seedlings have started to sprout (see p. 92). Circle of the Meidias Painter. Height 14 cms. Badisches Landesmuseum, Karlsruhe.

they symbolized a woman's body; the breaking of the pot was a sign that the body itself was disordered. Dr Reeder believes that the metaphor of woman as vessel had a deep significance for the ancient Greeks. It is well represented in two beautiful head vases, found in the same tomb at Vulci at the end of the nineteenth century. After their excavation they were separated, one going to Berlin and the other to St Petersburg, but they were reunited for the 'Pandora' exhibition in Basle.

The metaphor brings to women properties of a vessel or of a container. When one thinks about it, these connotations are protection, treasure, secrecy, but are also withholding, guile and concealment. These are qualities that have been attached to women through the years, and not only by the Greeks. They also involve the anxiety that surrounded women as givers of life, the apprehension about the life-giving process. After all, the Greeks were aware of the fact that they were unable to control sexuality, they could not control conception or fertility; they were aware that they could not control their children, and they were also aware that a mother's gift of life to her child is ultimately a gift of death; so the metaphor is an extremely powerful one.

In Greek weddings, all eyes were on the bride. At the crucial moment of the ceremony the bridegroom grasps her left wrist in a gesture of abduction or domination; but this is also known as the moment of seeing, since the veil is now lifted back from her face and she can look up at her new husband. The Greeks are very clear about the significance of this moment. Plato describes it in terms of magnetism: the bride's gaze radiates a desirability that makes the bridegroom respond to her with love, and she in turn looks back at him with the same obvious emotion. According to convention, Eros, son of Aphrodite, looks into the bride's eyes and so infuses her with this very desirability, even though this may well be the first time that she and her husband have ever met.

Men's Fear of Women in Love

The most fascinating, and at the same time insatiable, of all women was Eos, goddess of the dawn. In this painting by an unknown artist – he is generally known as the Christie Painter – she is depicted larger in size than the young hunter, probably Tithonos, whom she desires and pursues. Her hands are greedily outstretched to seize him, while he looks back in alarm. (This was a theme which reversed the usual subject of men chasing women, and was obviously a sexually intriguing subject.) Eos, we read, was so enamoured of Tithonos that she asked Zeus to grant him immortality, which the god obligingly did; but as the poor man got older and greyer

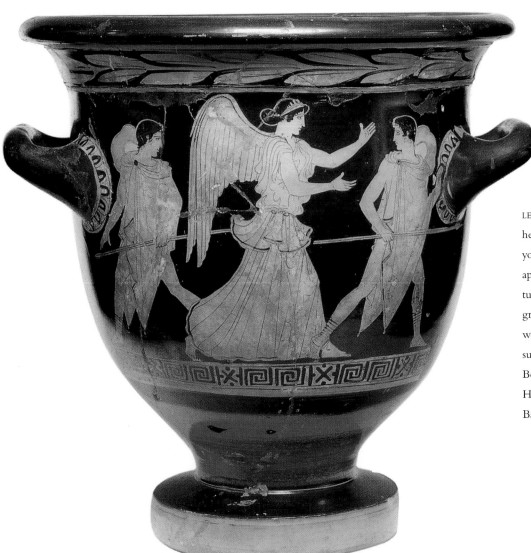

LEFT: Eos, the goddess of the dawn, is seen here with outstretched hands chasing the young hunter Tithonos. He looks back at her apprehensively, while his hunting companion turns to run in the other direction. Her greater size gives her a maternal quality, but a woman chasing young men for sexual pleasure gives the scene a sense of social taboo. Bell Krater by the Christie Painter. *c.* 440 BC. Height 37 cms. Baltimore Museum of Art, Baltimore, USA.

ABOVE: Amazon female warrior attacking a Greek, who is trying to protect himself with his raised shield. Although Plutarch never believed Homer's Amazon stories, recent discoveries have unearthed an ancient tribe in south-west Asia, who consisted of horse-women warriors. It is thought that the men, after many years in the saddle had lost their potency and the women had taken over. Ref: 1014. British Museum.

she realized, too late, that she should have stipulated eternal youth as well. Not surprisingly, she tired of the mumbling old man; first she shut him up, then turned him into a cicada. On a hot summer night in any Greek olive grove, you can still hear him trying to scratch his way out.

Eos was the sort of woman that Athenian men feared most; they were always terrified that, given the slightest opportunity, their women might revert to their primitive animal nature. This phobia was reflected even more strongly in another type of powerful woman – the Amazon, a frequent subject in Greek myth as well as in Greek art. According to Herodotus, the Amazons were a race of virgin warriors who joined the Trojans against the Greeks in the Trojan War. Their queen, Penthesilea, was killed in battle by Achilles, who fell in love with her as he stabbed her to death – an early example of the love–hate relationship between the sexes.

The Amazons were also depicted on one of the Seven Wonders of the Ancient World, the immense Mausoleum of Halicarnassus, fragments of which survive in the British Museum. One sculpture shows the Greeks dragging one Amazon off her horse and striking at another already fallen. Later, the Athenians added to this myth with the story of an Amazonian attack on Athens itself during the Golden Age. Military triumphs were best illustrated by showing a weaker enemy defeated; women, already feared by the Athenian men, made an ideal target.

There were other fearsome women too: Medusa the Gorgon, with writhing snakes instead of hair, the sight of whose face was alone enough to turn men to stone; Medea the enchantress, who left the court of her father Aeetes to help her lover Jason to find the Golden Fleece and who, when he betrayed and abandoned her, destroyed their children – the ultimate revenge of a woman scorned; the Maenads, who tattooed their bodies and held orgies on mountain tops, dancing round a huge stone in the shape of a phallus, with a man dressed in a goatskin who represented the god Pan.

The Phallic Symbol

A common sight in ancient Athens was a herm, a symbol of good luck dedicated to Hermes, god of travel (see figure on p. 99). Herms were usually set up beside roads, at boundaries and in front of houses. They normally took the form of the head

LEFT: This Greek funerary vase seems to show that despite past antagonisms between the sexes, real love can be shown at death. The dead man grasps his wife's hand, but she looks on the ground as she cannot see him. He, however, can see her and looks at her with great tenderness. He leans on a stick which is no longer visible as it was originally painted. Vase known as the 'Munchner Lekythos', 370–350 BC. Ref: GL 498. Munich Glyptothek Museum.

of the god Hermes surmounting a square, tapering pillar from which, half-way up, there projected an erect phallus. Hermes was the son of Zeus and Maia, daughter of Atlas. He was also the inventor of the lyre, which he presented to Apollo, god of music. The god is usually depicted carrying one, as can be seen in this kylix painting of a libation ceremony: the offering of drink as a sacrifice. The construction of the lyre is clearly visible here, its gut strings running down from the neck across the soundbox of tortoiseshell.

Zeus appointed Hermes messenger of the gods, giving him winged sandals for speed and a broad-brimmed hat as a protection from the sun on his extensive journeys. In Arcadia, Hermes had a son, Pan, who had the ears and legs of a goat. Pan was sexually insatiable: the nymph Syrinx threw herself into the river Ladon to escape his advances and was turned into a bed of reeds. Legend has it that it was from these that Pan made the first set of pan-pipes, which he then instructed the shepherds to play.

Soon after Plato's time the philosopher Diogenes wrote that Pan fell in love with another nymph, Echo – who may or may not have been the one who loved Narcissus – and desperately searched the countryside for her. Hermes took pity on his son and taught him the art of self-gratification, which Pan in turn taught to the shepherds. A sculpture (illustrated on p. 100) shows him in a state of sexual excitement as he teaches a young shepherd boy to play the pipes; in another, he satisfies his lust with a she-goat. This was the unbridled side of sex, which could

OPPOSITE: Arcadia in spring. A wooded and mountainous region on the west central Peloponnese, where Pan, with his nymphs and shepherds, held sway.

ABOVE: Marble 'herm' from Siphnos. *c.*520 BC. Ref: Ap3728. National Archaeological Museum, Athens.

LEFT: A rare white *kylix* of Apollo found at Delphi, where he had strong religious links through his oracles. The son of Zeus and Leto, he was born on the island of Delos, twin of his sister Artemis. Here he sits on a beautifully painted *diphros* (folding stool) pouring a libation from a *phiale*. He holds the lyre presented to him by Hermes (see p. 84) while a sacred raven looks on. The painting is of the highest quality – the toe of his sandal and the bird's tail giving balance to the whole composition by just breaking the circle. *c.* 470 BC. Delphi Museum.

TOP: Marble statue of Pan found in Herculaneum. 1st century AD. Ref: 27708. Archaeological Museum, Naples.

ABOVE: Priapic bronze figurine of Silenus found in Dodone in northern Greece. 535–525 BC. Ref: Carapenos 22. National Archaeological Museum, Athens.

RIGHT: Marble statue of Pan teaching Daphnis to play the pan-pipes. 2nd century Roman copy of a 2nd century BC Greek original. Archaeological Museum, Naples.

suddenly strike anyone with unexpected and frightening force. It was particularly dangerous to disturb Pan at mid-day, for he would then cause herds to stampede and visit dozing shepherds with appalling nightmares. The result in both cases would be the condition which still bears his name – panic.

Another creature which was half-way between a man and a beast – but not, like Pan, divine – was the satyr, who also wandered about the countryside chasing after nymphs and showing obvious indications of sexual arousal. A bronze figure of a satyr from about 530 BC is the best-selling postcard among tourists in Greece today. Almost indistinguishable from the satyrs in the earliest times was the race that was known as the Sileni; however, even Greek mythology did not really have enough capacity for both of these, and the name Silenus was therefore-

ABOVE: Mosaic of a pastoral scene with cow-herd playing the flute, with cattle from a Roman villa in Corinth, which is a version of a painting by Pausias, a distinguished Greek painter c. 360–330 BC. Ref: A610. Archaeological Museum, Corinth.

instead to the fat and rollicking attendant of Dionysus, the god of wine and debauchery.

Dionysus was another of the sons of Zeus, this time by a mortal woman – Semele, daughter of the King of Thebes. However, Zeus' jealous wife, Hera, determined to have her revenge, and, pretending to doubt whether Semele's lover was really her husband, suggested that she confirm the fact by asking him to appear in his true shape. Zeus did so and appeared as a thunderbolt, which unfortunately killed Semele; but he took from her womb the baby Dionysus, and had him brought up by Silenus and the nymphs.

An unusual temple was erected to Dionysus in about 300 BC on the sacred island of Delos. Known as the Stoibadeion, it has a rectangular front courtyard with, at each end, a pillar bearing a gigantic phallus. Only the truncated remains can be seen today, but on the front one of these pillars one can still see a relief carving of a cockerel, with a phallus for a head. On the sunlit side is a group of maenads with Dionysus; and opposite, in the shade, are the smaller figures of Silenus and Pan.

RIGHT: Marble statue of the 'Barberini' faun. This sleeping faun, the Roman equivalent of a Greek satyr, was probably carved by a Greek sculptor living in Rome around the first century AD. It was rediscovered during the Renaissance by one of the Barberni popes who refused to have it destroyed because of its beauty. Centuries later King Maximillian I of Bavaria and his son Ludwig, when bargaining with Pope Pius VII over territories with the other powers in Europe after the defeat of Napoleon, was asked by the Pope what he wanted in return for a particular favour. He replied, 'Your faun'. It still resides today in the Glyptothek Museum in Munich.

OPPOSITE: Part of the 'Temple of Dionysus' or the Stoibadeion, which originally was a rectangular exedra measuring 7.50 x 3.20 metres which had a pillar at both corners supporting an outsized phallus. The one shown has a large plinth on which can be seen the god Dionysos dancing with some Maenads. A resident called Carystios paid for the temple's construction in about 300 BC. Island of Delos, Greece.

7 *The Mutilation of the Herms*

In 415 BC, the Athenians decided to launch a vast expedition to Sicily, one of their richest and most important colonies. According to the historian Thucydides this was the idea of Alcibiades, who was anxious to show off his brilliance as a military leader – and also to lay his hands, as commander of the Athenian fleet, on the island's considerable wealth. He made, we are told, an astonishingly boastful speech to the Athenian assembly, reminding them of his success in the chariot races at the previous Olympic Games and his subsequent generosity to the city, and easily won their approval for the venture.

The following morning, however, the Athenians awoke to find that their herms had been deprived of their phalli overnight. They were not only shocked but also frightened: this violent attack on all their symbols of good luck, and especially of travel, was surely a dreadful omen for the coming expedition. The blame fell, somewhat illogically, on Alcibiades himself. He was known for his love of practical jokes, his disrespect for the 'divine mysteries' and his jealousy of those who shared his power; but as joint leader of the departing fleet – he was in fact to share the command with two other generals – he would hardly have contemplated an action which risked the cancellation of the entire operation.

Moreover, these wholesale amputations would have required a small regiment of perpetrators; Professor Keuls believes that they were the women of Athens themselves. Since it was the time of the annual Adonis festival, when the streets were anyway loud with wailing and smashing of pots, they would have been free to roam without attracting any particular attention. They were of course aware of the military and naval preparations in progress: shipyards were working day and night on the hundred triremes and vast numbers of merchant ships to carry stores and provisions, to say nothing of the 5,000 light-armed foot soldiers, known as hoplites. Professor Eva Keuls argues that this may therefore have been the first female protest against

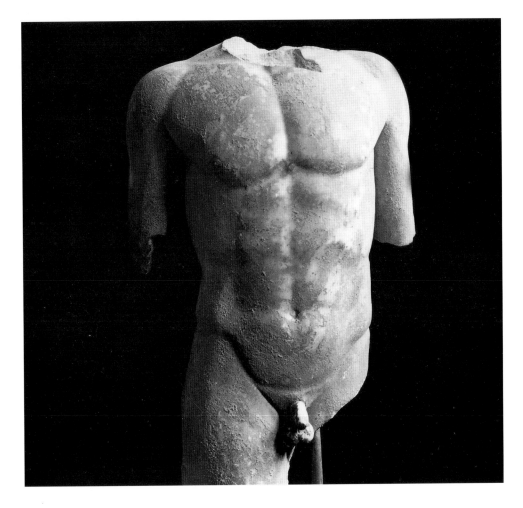

OPPOSITE: Statue of a Spartan warrior, possibly Leonidas, King of Sparta 487–480 BC. He bravely fought the Persian army under Xerxes at the pass of Thermopylae, but died outnumbered. 490–480 BC. Sparta Museum, Peloponnese, Greece.

LEFT: Male torso of a Spartan. 5th century BC. Sparta Museum, Peloponnese, Greece.

war. They had already had to endure years of fighting with Sparta; were their men really to set off again on yet another war? Enough was enough.

This theory certainly seems more likely than any other, but we shall probably never know for sure. Aristophanes, who mentions the affair in his *Lysistrata*, may have known who the culprits were, but he certainly gave no hint in his play. The mystery of the missing phalli must remain, like so many others in ancient history, unsolved.

The protest was unsuccessful and the expedition sailed. But the omens proved all too true. The Sicilian expedition was a fiasco. All the triremes were lost in the harbour of Syracuse, and most of the 40,000 Athenians were killed. The two other commanders, Demosthenes and Nicias, were put to death by the Syracusans. As for Alcibiades, he was summoned back to Athens to face trial. When the trireme arrived to fetch him, however, he jumped ship, crossed over in a small boat to the Peloponnese and sought refuge with his city's old enemy, the King of Sparta. While there, true to form, he seduced the Queen and was obliged to take flight once again – this time to another traditional enemy, Persia.

The defeat of the Sicilian expedition at Syracuse was the greatest that the Athenians had ever suffered and marked the beginning of the end of their empire,

RIGHT: Head of Alexander the Great. Late Hellenistic. 4th century AD. Glyptothek und Staatliche Antiken Sammlung, Munich.
OPPOSITE: Alexander the Great. Late Hellenistic. 4th century AD. Glyptothek und Staatliche Antiken Sammlung, Munich.

which now began its gradual decline. The end came seventy-seven years later, in 338 BC, when King Philip of Macedonia killed over a thousand Athenians at the Battle of Chaeronea. This marked the collapse of Athens as a military power and changed the whole face of Greece.

But now, from this northern Kingdom of Macedonia, there rose a new star which outshone all before it: Philip's son, Alexander the Great. He continued his father's conquest of the rest of Greece, but went far beyond – through Persia to what is now Afghanistan, and to the very confines of India. Athens itself he spared, out of respect for the superb culture that had so inspired him and for his own tutor Aristotle.

When Alexander reached Athens he is said to have offered the famous philosopher Diogenes – who lived in a large barrel – anything he wanted. 'Get out of my light' was his reply, since Alexander happened to be standing between him and the sun. But Alexander's own sun was to set all too soon. By the time he was only thirty-one he had conquered most of the known world, from Egypt to India, and complained that he had no worlds left to conquer. Two years later, while he was on his way back to the West, his lover Hephaestion suddenly died. Alexander was totally devastated, mourning for three days over the body. Soon afterwards, when he reached Babylon, he followed Hephaistion to the grave, probably from dysentery after drinking tainted water but possibly from poison. His young son was murdered soon afterwards, and his vast empire collapsed.

Alexander's death marked the end of the golden age of ancient Greece. But by now new legions were on the march, legions from a city-state more determined and dynamic than any which had gone before – Rome.

8 *The Etruscans*

The early arrival of Greek culture on the Italian peninsula had an immediate influence on the mysterious local race of the Etruscans and, through them, on their neighbours living in Rome – at that time still little more than a village on the river Tiber. The origins of the Etruscans are still uncertain; even their language is not yet properly understood. At an early stage, however, they seem to have adopted some of the Greek gods, and certain of the Greek religious customs. Their supreme deity was female: Uni, whom the Romans took over as Juno, goddess of women and birth.

One morning in early April 1927, the English writer D. H. Lawrence set off from Tarquinia in central Italy with an American friend Earl Brewster, a painter, to see and later write about his experiences in *Etruscan Places*:

'Tarquinia is only about three miles from the sea ... We descend in the bare place, which seems to expect nothing. On the left is a beautiful stone palazzo, on the right is a café upon the low ramparts above the gate ... In the warm April morning the stony little town seems half asleep ... The slight sense of desertedness is everywhere...'

Lawrence and Brewster find a guide to show them the painted tombs:

'... which are the real fame of Tarquinia. After lunch we set out, climbing to the top of the town, and passing through the south-west gate ... The Etruscans never buried their dead within the city walls ... we see ... a little hood of masonry with an iron gate, covering a little flight of steps leading down into the ground ... The lamp begins to shine and smell, then to shine without smelling: the guide opens the iron gate, and we descend the steep steps down into the tomb.'

ABOVE: 'Tomb of the Bulls' with the main rear wall fresco with one of two doors shown. In the top frieze a bull with the face of Achelous. He took the form of a bull after losing a fight with Hercules, who then took one of his horns, which may be the sexual symbolism behind the painting – (see pp. 111 and 113 for detail of this panel). *c.* 550 BC. 'Tomb of the Bulls', Tarquinia, Italy.

'One of the most famous tombs at this far-off end of the necropolis is the Tomb of the Bulls. It contains what the guide calls: *un po' di pornografico!* – but a very little. The [guide] … informs us that this is one of the oldest tombs of all, and I believe him, for it looks so to me …The ancients saw … the everlasting wonder in things …They were like children: but they had the force, the power and the sensual knowledge of true adults … Even the two bits of '*pornografico*' in the Tomb of the Bull are not two little dirty drawings. Far from it …The drawings have the same naïve wonder in them as the rest, the same archaic innocence, accepting life, knowing all about it, and *feeling* the meaning…'

Today, the tombs are lit by electricity. The colours in the tomb of the Bulls are as striking as those remembered by Lawrence in the tomb of the Leopards (see end-papers), named for the two figures of leopards on the wall. Here Lawrence really felt that there was a people that he could identify with. He admired the liveliness of the flute player and the harp player. The woman with fair hair, who Lawrence thought might be a prostitute or hetaira, in fact may well be the occupant of the tomb's wife. She pinches his skin in a familiar manner. He is carrying an egg, probably a sign of fertility; nowhere in this tomb can you see any symbol of death. The egg is also a symbol in the tomb of the Diver, again symbolizing the continuity of life.

BELOW: 'Tomb of the Bulls'. Detail of end wall (see p. 112) showing a mythological scene of Achilles on far left, in helmet and loincloth, lying in wait to kill Troilus, who approaches naked on his tall pale horse. The panel below shows trees hung with sashes and wreaths of the dead. The tomb measures 4.31 x 4.50 x 2.52 metres high. *c.*550 BC. 'Tomb of the Bulls', Tarquinia, Italy.

OPPOSITE: A detail of a wall fresco painting in 'The Tomb of the Bulls' (see p. 112) of two men and a woman. One man is kneeling while the indistinct shape of the woman (always painted much lighter than the men), is lying on her back, while the other man, standing, makes love to her. This is counterbalanced by another erotic painting (see p. 111) on the right side of this frieze. These images have not yet been interpreted, but they are thought to have something to do with warding off the 'evil eye' – in the same way as the phallus did in ancient Greece and Rome. *c.* 550 BC. 'Tomb of the Bulls', Tarquinia, Italy.

LEFT: Woman dancing in a lively fresco in the 'Tomb of the Jugglers'. *c.* 530 BC. Tarquinia, Italy.

Lawrence admired above everything the feeling of joy and of life reflected in Etruscan culture and art. He summed up his experience:

'If you want uplift, go to the Greek and the Gothic. If you want mass, go to the Roman. But if you love the odd spontaneous forms that are never to be standardized, go to the Etruscans.'

One wonders whether the writer of *Lady Chatterley's Lover* knew of the Greek historian Theopompus (*c.* 378–300 BC). What he wrote concerning the Etruscans and their love lives was paraphrased by Athenaeus 600 years later:

'The Etruscans were decadent and fond of luxury. The women may appear naked and exercise with the men or with each other; they are shared among the men and dine

ABOVE: 'Tomb of the Whipping' fresco of two naked men; the one on the left wears a wreath while the one on the right has a red sash; both are whipping the indistinct form of a woman in the middle, possibly as part of an unknown Dionysian rite. It measures 5.30 x 4.50 x 2 metres high. *c.* 490 BC. 'Tomb of the Whipping', Tarquinia, Italy.

not with their husbands but any men present, and they are beautiful and enjoy drinking. All their babies are reared in a communal way without even knowing who their fathers are.

Etruscans are shameless and quite open about the master of the house's affairs, because after they have stopped drinking at dinner parties, servants – with the lights still burning! – introduce sometimes female prostitutes, sometimes very beautiful boys, also sometimes their wives; and after they have enjoyed these, the servants introduce lusty young men, who in their turn consort with them. This occurs with or without screens for discretion; and although the Etruscans consort eagerly with women, prefer boys and striplings for they are very good-looking and keep their bodies smooth.'

What seems to have scandalized Theopompus was what he saw as the 'decadence' of Etruscan women, in fact simply their ease in their relations with their husbands. True, respectable Greek women were not seen at symposia, but for him to be shocked by their behaviour with prostitutes and boys after a drinking party seems to be an example of the Greek pot calling the Etruscan kettle black. The right of Etruscan women to raise children without their husbands' formal recognition is, according to Lavissa Bonfante, 'probably connected with their right to own property'. He also describes Theopompus as drawing 'the worst possible conclusions from what he heard and may have seen about Etruscan women'.

Bonfante stresses the importance of couples in Etruria – 'where the family counted for more than the single male citizen' – compared with that of the Greeks and the Romans. In one terracotta group we see an Etruscan couple naked under a single toga – a notion quite foreign to Greek art. The Greeks may have shown mythical couples – Orpheus and Eurydice, Zeus and Hera, Artemis and Actaeon – but these were rarely naked together; in fact Actaeon, who while hunting inadvertently saw Artemis bathing, was turned by her into a stag and torn to shreds by his hounds.

Besides owning property, Etruscan women had luxurious tombs and sarcophagi inscribed with their own names. Women also had first and family names; in fact, because of the importance of the family unit, it is thought the Etruscans were probably the first to use a family name.

With her contented and enigmatic smile, the Etruscan wife on the sarcophagus seems to have a bond of love with her husband, whose arm is around her. Herodotus, the Greek historian, thought the Etruscans came from Asia Minor; certainly the curled toes of her slippers have an eastern look. Her elaborate footwear emphasizes her importance, compared to her husband with his sturdy bare feet.

BELOW: Terracotta sarcophagus of a reclining Etruscan husband and wife. *c.* 530 BC. Louvre Museum, Paris.

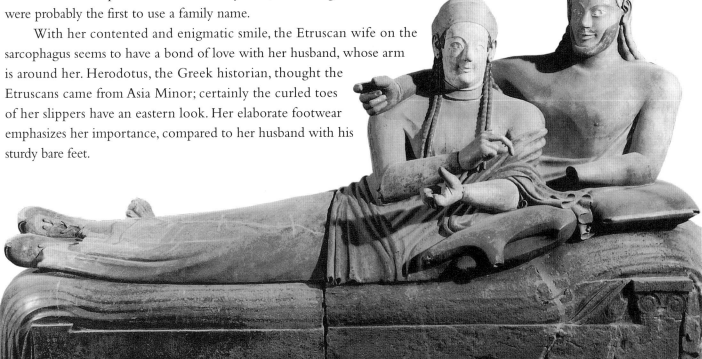

9 *The Romans and their Gods*

BELOW: Ithyphallic Mercury. He is carrying
his caduceus (or wand) in his right hand, and
a money bag in his left, as he was the Roman
god of commerce and gain (the equivalent of
the Greek god Hermes). There are even tiny
wings on his heels, which look a little small
to propel him and his 'good-luck' phallus. *c.*
60 AD. Wall painting, Pompeii.

The first King of Rome was an Etruscan, Tarquin I, crowned in 616 BC. He brought many of his people's social customs to Rome, the relative freedom of Roman women in later times being one of many Etruscan legacies. The Roman goddess Juno – originally the Etruscan Uni – is another, although she was also identified with the Greek Hera. Juno was one of the three principal deities worshipped by the Romans on the Capitoline hill, the other two being her husband Jupiter, corresponding to the Greek Zeus; and Minerva, goddess of wisdom, identified with Athena. The Greek war god Ares became Mars; Aphrodite became Venus, and her son Eros became Cupid.

Minor gods also were adapted and assimilated, among these the legendary Sibyls, prophetesses of the ancient world. The most renowned was the Cumaean Sibyl, originally a woman named Herophile. She was loved by Apollo, who offered to give her whatever she wished. She picked up a handful of sand and asked to live for as many years as the number of grains she held. The god granted her wish – but, like Tithonos, she was not granted eternal youth and grew for ever older and uglier. An awe-inspiring tunnel deep in the rocks of Cumae, near modern-day Naples, was her home. The Sibyls were the first of a long tradition of ecstatic female prophetesses, like the famous Cassandra who was generally regarded as an 'inspired' prophetess, uttering her oracles in a trance-like state. Later they were believed to have foretold the arrival of Christ, and so were the only group of females from the pagan

days to survive into Christian mythology. Michelangelo's marvellous fresco of the Cumaean Sibyl in the Sistine Chapel in Rome shows her uttering her prophecy.

Another minor god the Romans inherited from Greece was Priapus, the wickedly promiscuous god of fertility whose paternity was attributed to Dionysus (amongst others) with whom he shared an Asiatic origin, and in whose retinue he was included. The Roman poet Horace sums up the way the ancient Italians thought about Priapus, as a god of good luck or even a kind of scarecrow who kept away thieves and birds:

> *A sculptor once saw me where once I stood*
> *once a useless piece of wood,*
> *Now scared birds dart from leaves*
> *while my biggest stump scares the thieves.*

ABOVE: Terracotta figurine of Juno with a peacock (see p. 118). She was the consort of Jupiter, goddess of marriage and maternity. Roman 1st century AD from Tunis.

RIGHT: The minor god Priapus weighing his phallus (see p. 121). Front door hallway. *c.* 50 AD. House of the Vettii, Pompeii.

PREVIOUS PAGE (p. 119): Interior of the prophetess Sibyl's cave near Cumae. The poet Virgil even spoke of this cave of the prophetess, but no one could find it. It was not until 1932 that it was discovered, although, mysteriously, no trace was found of any remains in the grotto. The tunnel carved out of the solid rock is about 5 metres high and 132 metres long. *c.* 550 BC Cumae, Campania, Italy.

Love for Sale

Two and a half thousand years later, old Priapus is still causing ribald laughter and, perhaps, bringing good luck to the tourists who come and see the paintings in a Roman villa in Pompeii. This Priapus (on p. 120) is even weighing his phallus, perhaps measuring the amount of good luck he can bring, and his power to ward off the evil eye. The owner of the house wanted it to be the first thing the visitor would see, so he placed it in the hall by the front door, bringing good luck to all who entered.

Pompeii was a town, near Naples, which lay under the shadow of Vesuvius. In AD 79 it was completely buried by a cataclysmic eruption of the volcano. It was not until 1748, however, that the first serious excavations began there, and what the diggers uncovered was a city which had been frozen in time. This

ABOVE: Pompeii from the top of the Gate of Vesuvius, showing much of the already excavated city which was laid out in the Greek manner with long narrow residential blocks transversed by narrow access streets. As it was in 79 AD. Pompeii.

astonishing discovery has given us an unrivalled view of the streets, the houses, the public buildings and forums of an ancient Italian city; and it gives an uniquely detailed picture of the daily life of its people. But would Rome have been similar to Pompeii at this time? Dr Mary Beard thinks so, and takes us down a Roman street in about 100 BC:

> 'Compared with Rome, Athens was a tiny place, as it was just one little city state. Rome on the other hand was a vast multicultural cosmopolitan empire which covered the whole of the known world. Now, despite that difference, there were all sorts of things that were quite similar in terms of sexual practice and ideas about love that united Rome with Athens.
>
> Rome, which had conquered Greece, took over some of the morals and the assumptions about sexual behaviour that the Greeks had had before. I think if we

OPPOSITE: Courtyard of the 'House of Venus' from the peristyle. At the time of the eruption of Vesuvius in 79 AD, this house belonging to a wealthy family was being restored by them; Venus on her shell is in the shade on the left of the picture. AD 79. Pompeii.

ABOVE: Mural in the 'House of Venus', with *trompe-l'oeil* fountain with birds. 79 AD. Pompeii.

ABOVE: A stone phallus to bring good luck on a wall at the corner of Via Stabiana. *c.* 10 AD. Pompeii.

were to visit Rome, what would strike us, even more forcefully than Athens, would be the extreme prominence of phalli, penises, male genitals all over the place. Little boys wore phalli round their necks, and there were phalli hung up in Pompeian houses with bells on them and wings. There were phalli outside the doors. There were phalli on the street corner. There were phalli in places that we would have banned in our own culture, but in Rome they were part of every day life.

Now why was that? Why does a culture like Rome have erotic scenes even on its bedside table lights? I think we can't answer that question by examining the range of things that you saw if you walked down the Roman street, as they very much fitted in with how Roman men were ideally supposed to behave. The ideal man in Rome was a fighter; he was a public speaker, and he was essentially a penetrator. He did not have to restrict his sexual behaviour and his sexual relations to relations with women. What was crucial was that he did not himself become penetrated. To be penetrated as a Roman man was a sign of effeminacy, a kind of oriental decadence; it was a sign that you were the kind of man who shaved their underarms and plucked the hairs off their legs and wore perfume.

One of the interesting things about the Roman language is that the word for sword in Latin, gladius, is the same as one of the words you could use for penis. And in some ways if you're looking for a mythical tie-up with all this, you'd see the Roman man as being a bit like the god Pan, a half animal, half male creature who stalks the wilds outside the city and himself penetrates anything

ABOVE: Phallus carved in a light coloured rock, called travertine, which is made by deposits from springs. It bears the inscription 'HIC HABITAT FELICITAS' – 'Here dwells happiness' – another good luck sign found above a bakery. Felicity of course could have been the baker's wife! 1st century AD. Archaeological Museum, Naples.

LEFT: Phallus carved into the wall of a shop in Pompeii – bringing luck to the shopkeeper's family and no doubt the clients as well. 60 AD. Pompeii.

RIGHT: Fresco on the hall wall in the 'Lupanara' of a Priapic figure of a young man with two phalli – maybe one for show and one for luck! The 'Lupanara', a brothel in Pompeii. 1st century AD. Pompeii.

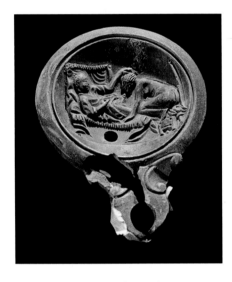

ABOVE: Oil table light depicting fellatio. 1st century AD from Pompeii. Archaeological Museum, Naples.

that there is in sight – preferably nymphs, but if there's no nymphs then a goat will do. So the Roman man has an image of himself as someone who must live up to that penetrative ideal.'

In the entrance hall of a brothel in Pompeii is a faded painting of a man holding a 'double penis' – perhaps one for action and one for luck. This town of about 12,000 inhabitants had 34 brothels. A Latin word for a brothel is *lupanara*, from lupa, she-wolf, which also means prostitute. Perhaps the girls used to wolf-whistle at prospective clients from their upper balcony. Another name for a prostitute was *nonaria*, meaning 'ninth hour'. The Romans counted hours from dawn, so this meant four in the afternoon, opening time for the lupanara.

The brothel had ten rooms, five on each floor, and was used by the poorer or slave classes. The other pictures probably advertised various specialities on offer to clients. The beds were all built into the walls and had a mattress for comfort. According to the graffiti found scribbled on the walls it seems that many of the girls working there were from Greece or the Far East. Brothels were heavily taxed under a law enacted a few years earlier by the emperor Caligula.

The Banning of the Bacchanalia

The well known myth of 'Roman orgies' probably stems from a law passed in 186 BC by the senate banning any further Bacchanalia. These were the mysteries of a fanatical and mystical cult of Bacchus, god of wine. They were celebrated, generally at night, by women in wild frenzies of religious and sexual arousal.

The Roman historian Livy recounts a strange story of whores, blackmail, sadomasochism and murder that was scandalizing Rome at the time. A young man called Aebutius had a stepfather who wanted to blackmail him into signing over his property. The boy's mother, who was under the stepfather's influence, persuaded

BELOW: Painting on the wall inside the 'Lupanara' of a position very rarely depicted in Greek erotic art. From the 'Lupanara' brothel in Pompeii. 1st century AD. Pompeii.

her son to prepare for the Bacchanalia. Aebutius jokingly told his girlfriend what he was going to do, and she was horrified. She told him she had once gone to the Bacchanalia herself where, she said, the priests led young men – always under 20 years old – like beasts to the altar. She then describes the orgy in her own words:

'There were drums, cymbals and hymns so no one could hear the young man's cries as he was violated. At the start, the shrine had been reserved for women only, but a woman from Campania had changed the whole ritual, ostensibly at the command of the gods, by initiating two young men – her sons. Then it was open to both sexes and the men were guilty of more immoral acts among themselves than with the women.

The women dressed as Bacchantes and, with their hair unbound and carrying flaming sulphur torches, they went down to the Tiber to round up the initiates. Anyone who was slow to join in was slaughtered in sacrifice like a beast. The society had a huge membership, almost a third of the population, and many of them of noble birth.'

On hearing this dreadful story of the acts in which he had nearly been forced to take part, Aebutius told his aunt, who told a consul. During the ensuing trials the charges that revolted the senate more than accusations of lust and murder were those of fabrication of evidence and forging of wills. These were crimes against the state, punishable by death.

BELOW: Paintings from a brothel wall showing various positions of lovemaking – *pour encourager les clients*! The illustration shows the prostitute still wearing her brassière, with an inscription above the scene in Latin 'LENTE IMPELLE' – 'push slowly'. 1st century AD. Ref: 27690. Archaeological Museum, Naples.

OPPOSITE: Interior of the 'Lupanara' showing an erotic painting above the door into one of the small rooms for the prostitutes or 'nonariae' – 'the ninth hour girls'. Also visible is the stone and plaster bed-bunk which would be covered with a mattress. (see p. 127). The 'Lupanara' brothel. 1st century AD. Pompeii.

10 *The Women of Rome*

The story of Aebutius and the Bacchanalia sheds an interesting light on the relative independence of the women of ancient Rome. They had a great deal more freedom than Greek women, and even had some control over their dowries – which might be huge, thanks to the riches that flooded into the city from the foreign conquests of a growing empire. A Roman girl might or might not be tutored at home rather than go to school with her brothers; but she was never, like her Greek counterpart, held a virtual prisoner inside the house. When she grew up she would dine out in mixed company, discussing current affairs on equal terms with the men around her.

As early as 195 BC, the women of Rome gave proof of the power they enjoyed when they came together to protest against what was known as the Oppian Law, a sumptuary law forbidding them from wearing gold ornaments and expensively dyed clothes. After ten years of these restrictions they had had enough; they streamed into the Forum in their thousands and besieged the Senate. The law was repealed by Cato the Elder, and the Roman women once again started spending.

Rome's full exposure to Greek culture was partly the result of the plundering of Greece. In 146 BC the Roman senate launched an expedition against Corinth. The city was totally ransacked, and its gold, statues and other works of art taken to Rome. Corinth did not recover from this for over 100 years. When the Roman general Aemilius Paulus pillaged Macedonia, the former kingdom of Alexander the Great, he brought back such a quantity of sculptures, statues and paintings, together with slaves, that it took three days for the triumphal procession to pass through Rome.

The Romans eagerly seized Greek statues of Aphrodite, goddess of love, and of her son Eros, and copied them. In fact we know most Greek statues only from Roman copies. Peter Rockwell, a sculptor now living in Rome, explains:

OPPOSITE: Statue of a Roman matron who is depicted as possibly giving an offering to the gods. 1st century BC. Archaeological Museum, Naples.

130

Eros, whom the Romans called Cupid, is the messenger of love and he is drawing his bow, arming himself to shoot an arrow at us to make us fall in love. The original of this statue is by Lysippus, who was the court sculptor for Alexander the Great in the 4th century BC, so it is very possible that General Paulus brought the original to Rome from Macedonia. The Roman sculptor, I suspect, is more interested in the beautiful body of the young boy, than he is in the bow or Cupid arming himself.

The same sensuality can also be seen in the statue of Cupid and Psyche (p. 135) – Eros in love with the human soul. Notice the two slightly soft and pudgy tummies, showing the Roman view of male beauty as something as soft and rather closer to female beauty – it's certainly not the muscular young men of the Greek concept of beauty. It's a statue which was probably kept in a private garden, not a public statue, the sort of thing that you would see when you went for dinner at a senator's house or a wealthy person's house; it is, though, a tremendously sentimental view of love.'

OPPOSITE: Temple of Apollo showing three of the seven remaining Archaic Doric columns (see p. 132). 550 BC. Corinth.

ABOVE: Cupid stretching his bow. Roman copy of a Greek original by Lysippus 350–300 BC. Capitoline Museum, Rome.

ABOVE: Head of an unknown young Roman man. Hellenistic. Archaeological Museum, Naples.

Romans in Love

The Romans' approach to homosexual love was very different to that of the Greeks. They had no interest in winning young boys by influencing them mentally and spiritually; they simply wanted to seduce them as quickly as possible, if necessary by the simplest method of all – straight purchase. Cato – he who had reluctantly repealed the Oppian law – was shocked to discover that a good-looking young boy could be sold for as much as a talent, the price of a small farm.

For heterosexual young men of independent means, the first century before Christ was a time of cynicism and extramarital affairs. Gaius Valerius Catullus came to Rome from Verona in 60 BC when he was only twenty. His poems are concise and often blunt, and have much in common with modern sensibility. The love of his life, whom he called Lesbia, was in fact the formidable and self-willed Clodia Metella, wife of the politician Metellus Celer.

Some of Catullus' poems are full of irreverent humour, and some have homoerotic elements, like this one.

> A matter for mirth, Cato, and a smile
> worth your attention, you'll laugh
> you'll laugh as you love your Catullus, Cato
> listen – a matter for more than a smile!
> Just now I found a young boy stuffing his girl,
> I rose, naturally, and (with a nod to Venus)
> fell and transfixed him there
> with a good stiff prick, like his own.

But Catullus' obsession was his Lesbia ...

> Lesbia says she'd rather marry me than anyone,
> though Jupiter himself came asking, or so she says,
> but what a woman tells her lover in desire
> should be written out on air and running water.

... and her outrageous conduct.

> Lesbia, our Lesbia, the same old Lesbia,
> Caelius,★ she whom Catullus loved once
> more than himself and more than his own,
> loiters at the crossroads and in the back streets
> ready to toss off the magnanimous sons of Rome.

★(Caelius Rufus succeeds Catullus as Lesbia's lover and is similarly cast off by her.)

LEFT: Cupid and Psyche embracing (see p. 133). 1st century AD. Capitoline Museum, Rome.

This accusation against her sexual behaviour is underlined in a courtroom speech by Cicero, one of the great orators of the day, who was defending a young trainee lawyer against Clodia Metella. He harshly attacks her conduct in the seaside town of Baiae, near Naples:

'Yes, Baiae does not simply tell us a tale, but rings with the report that there is one woman so deeply sunk in her vicious depravities that she no longer even bothers to seek privacy and darkness and the usual veil of discretion to cover her lusts. On the contrary she actually exults in displaying the most foully lecherous goings on amid

the widest publicity and in the glaring light of day ... If a woman who has no husband throws open her home to every debauchee and publicly leads the life of a whore; if she makes a habit of being entertained by men who are total strangers; if she pursues this mode of existence in the city, in her own gardens, among the crowds at Baiae; if in fact she behaves in such a way that not only her general demeanour but also her dress and associates, her hot eyes and uninhibited language, her embraces and kisses, her beach parties, all show that she is not only a prostitute, but a lewd and depraved prostitute at that; if a young man should happen to be found in the company of such a woman, then surely, Lucius Herennius, you would agree that this was not so much adultery as just plain sex – not an outrage to chastity, but mere satisfaction of appetite.'

Baiae seems to have been like a combination of Saint-Tropez and Malibu rolled into one. Sex was no more than a pastime, not to be considered an ennobling experience. In fact, for the Romans, love did not make you better; it made you worse. The Roman comedies of Plautus are full of characters in love – young men, witless young men who need the help of their slaves to extract money from their parsimonious fathers to carry on their affairs. Love has made them the slaves of their mistresses – the very opposite of the independence that the Romans held dear.

So what could you expect if you were getting married in Rome? Love was certainly not the motive, it was far too frivolous a reason for entering anything as serious as marriage. Marriage was about money, it was about political alliances. People got divorced when the political winds changed – quite regularly, in fact. That is not to say that you might not love your wife or your wife might not love you. The great general Pompey (Gnaeus Pompeius Magnus) was certainly very much in love with his wife, who died in childbirth in 54 BC. Her name was Julia, the feminine form of the name of her illustrious father Julius Caesar, who was also a general, and who was to defeat Pompey in a power struggle for the empire.

The Great Lover-Generals

In the 50s BC Julius Gaius Caesar was governor of the Roman province of Gaul, roughly equivalent to modern France. He was the talk of Rome for both his military and his amorous exploits, and was regarded as a dandy who, besides spending his own fortune had also spent that of his wife. Not only was he called 'Queen of Bithynia' by the senate, because of his alleged affair with the king of that province, but he also enjoyed an almost legendary success with women. In fact he is reputed to have seduced most of the wives of his generals and even of his close friends, and was referred to behind his back as 'the husband of every woman and the wife of every man'. To commemorate the military success of his campaigns, Caesar commissioned the magnificent statue of the Dying Gaul. Clearly the sculptor of this extraordinarily powerful piece, and perhaps Caesar himself, were considerably more interested in the magnificent body of the Gaulish warrior, who is committing suicide

OPPOSITE: Statue of a Gaul holding his dead wife and about to commit suicide. Based on a sculpture by Epionos c. 230 BC, and probably commissioned by Julius Caesar and copied in c. 45 BC. Palazzo Altemps, Rome.

rather than be taken into slavery, than in the rag-doll depiction of his dead wife.

'I cannot imagine' said Cicero, 'when I see Caesar's thinning hair so carefully arranged and spot him adjusting it with one finger, that it should enter the thoughts of such a man to subvert the Roman state'; but subvert it he did. After the death of his wife Julia the tenuous relationship between himself and his son-in-law Pompey broke down completely; civil war was the result. In 49 BC Caesar's army, although easily outnumbered, inflicted a decisive defeat over Pompey in northern Greece. Pompey fled to Egypt; Caesar followed. When he stepped ashore at Alexandria, the Egyptians – who had no doubt where their best interests lay – presented him with the mummified head of his enemy.

Caesar now installed himself in the royal palace at Alexandria. At that time Egypt was still an independent kingdom, ruled jointly by its twenty-one-year-old queen, Cleopatra, and her brother Ptolemy XIII, who was six years younger than she. Each had their own group of advisers, but relations between the two could hardly have been worse. Caesar, adopting the old 'divide and rule' technique, began negotiating with Ptolemy.

Cleopatra, seeing that decisive action was necessary if she was to maintain her position, had herself wrapped in a carpet and smuggled through her brother's military guard into the presence of Caesar, who immediately fell in love with her. As were so many of the children of the Egyptian pharaohs, Cleopatra was the product of an incestuous marriage, and her portrait on coins suggests that she may not have been the fabulous beauty that Shakespeare and others have led us to believe; there is, however, no doubt that she was highly intelligent – she is said to have been an excellent mathematician and she was allegedly fluent in nine languages. Despite her affair with Caesar – and, later, her far more serious one with Antony – she does not appear to have been generally promiscuous. She probably agreed to become Caesar's mistress as much for political reasons as for any other; and for him, too, notwithstanding his initial infatuation with this brilliant young girl, power was always far more important than love.

For Ptolemy and his advisers, the occupation of the royal palace by Caesar was clearly not to be tolerated; and in February of 47 BC Pothinus the Eunuch – who, since Ptolemy himself was still a

BELOW: This huge cedar barge was discovered in 1954 next to the Great Pyramid of Khufu at Giza, and although made 2,500 years before Cleopatra's barge, the size and style would not have been that much different, only hers was much more luxurious. 43 metres long. *c.* 2530 BC. Solar Boat Museum, Giza.

minor, was titular Regent of Egypt – ordered an armed blockade. But Caesar had his own army, of 3,200 legionaries and 800 cavalry; and a fierce battle ensued, during which the Romans accidentally set fire to part of the great Library of Alexandria – the most important in antiquity. But the Romans, heavily outnumbered, soon found themselves surrounded, and Caesar was obliged to swim from the harbour mole to the Pharos – itself one of the Seven Wonders of the Ancient World – which, if captured, would control the harbour and thus prevent the landing of the relief force from Syria, in which lay his only hope of deliverance. (During the swim he lost his cloak, which was taken as a trophy by the Egyptians.) He and Cleopatra were saved, only just in time, by the arrival of the Syrian reinforcements.

So Caesar emerged victorious, Pothinus was beheaded on his orders, while Ptolemy fled for his life, only to be drowned soon afterwards in the Nile. Cleopatra now ruled supreme in Egypt. To placate the priests, she followed the old tradition and married a still younger brother – he was just eleven – who took the title of Ptolemy XIV. This did not however prevent her from going for a cruise up the Nile with Caesar and becoming pregnant by him.

Cleopatra's palace has recently been discovered beneath the harbour waters in Alexandria. So have the remains of the Pharos.

After Caesar's assassination in 44 BC his adopted son Octavian and his close friend Mark Antony divided the Empire between them. The western half went to Octavian, the eastern – including Egypt – to Antony. Before long he too had fallen under the spell of the extraordinary young queen, who in the fullness of time was to bear him twins, a boy and a girl. But whereas for Julius Caesar Cleopatra had been little more than a political tool and a delightful plaything, for Antony she became an all-consuming passion, to the point where he could no longer bring himself to leave Egypt and the oriental luxury with which he was surrounded. War between himself and Octavian soon became inevitable and at the naval battle of Actium – near Levkas in north-western Greece – his fleet was utterly destroyed. He returned, broken, to Alexandria, where one of the world's most famous love affairs ended as dramatically and extravagantly as it had begun. Antony fell on his sword; Cleopatra is said to have had an asp – or perhaps a sacred cobra whose fatal bite was believed to ensure immortality – smuggled into her chamber in a basket of figs, and held it to her breast. The snake did its work quite quickly.

On Cleopatra's death, Octavian declared the end of the pharaohs and of the Ptolemaic dynasties, with Egypt becoming part of the Roman Empire. He then returned in triumph to Rome, where he was awarded the title of Augustus and additionally declared himself imperator or Emperor. Cleopatra's dream of becoming Empress of the world was never realized, but her wish for immortality was granted. The loves and the fame of the last queen of Egypt shine undiminished to the present day.

TOP: Coin showing the head of Cleopatra – *Kleopatra VII. c. 34 BC.* British Museum.

ABOVE: Reverse of coin showing the head of Mark Antony. *c. 34 BC.* British Museum.

11 *The God-Emperor's Scandalous Daughter*

'Caesar to Stephanus, greetings. I have freed this city and recommended it to Antony. This one city, out of all the cities of Asia, I have taken for my own. I wish these people to be protected as my own townsmen. I shall be watching to see that you carry out my recommendation to the full.'

This inscription by Octavius Caesar is carved on the wall of the theatre of the magnificent marble-built city of Aphrodisias in Asia Minor, which – thanks almost entirely to the efforts of the later Professor Kenan Erim – now ranks with Ephesus as the most fascinating classical site in all Turkey. Its severe tone reflects the authority of the man who was about to become the first Roman Emperor, and who later would be revered as a god in his own right; but to anyone who has ever visited the city, his admiration comes as no surprise. Not only was the city, as its name implies, sacred to Aphrodite; it lay at the foot of a mountain which produced, with that of Carrera, the most exquisite marble in the entire Mediterranean world. This in turn had produced a school of sculpture that lasted for some five centuries, producing works of art of the highest quality that were exported throughout the Empire.

John Julius Norwich describes his first impressions of the city:

'I shall never forget my first arrival at this extraordinary city of the goddess of love. Professor Kenan Erim opened the door of the guarded compound to reveal a courtyard where sculpture after sculpture, all recently excavated from the surrounding site, stood around as if to greet me. The evening star, the

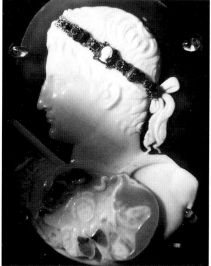

ABOVE: Three layer sardonyx cameo of Augustus wearing the aegis of Minerva and sword belt. His laurel wreath was replaced in the Middle Ages by the jewelled head-band. *c.* 16 AD. Ref: GR 1865.5–7.484. British Museum, London.

bedtime star and so Aphrodite's own, could clearly be seen before the moon was up, and despite a failed generator, Kenan Erim took me round his magnificent finds by candlelight.'

Many sculptures from Aphrodisias were shipped to Rome. From the masons' marks on the great monument, the Altar of Peace, made for the new emperor Augustus, it is clear that Greeks and Italians worked together to create it. At the front is the Mother Goddess in a world representing the productivity and fertility of the new empire that peace (and the emperor) had brought about. It is worth noticing, in addition, that this work completely lacks the sensuousness that

LEFT: The main frieze from the Altar of Peace showing Augustus on the extreme left with four Flammian Priests wearing spiked helmets in the centre and Agrippa on the extreme right. It was not until the 1930s that all the fragments were pieced together, and its historical importance realized. Museum of the Ara Pacis, Rome.

is normally such a feature of Aphrodisian sculpture. It is intended as a simple illustration of the benefits of peace and just government. Along the side we see the figures of the new Emperor and his family – including his grandchildren – proceeding on their way to perform a sacrifice to the gods. Dr Susan Fischler has an interesting comment about this:

ABOVE: Rare bust of Livia, wife of Augustus in green basalt. 1st century AD. Ref: Ma 1233. Louvre Museum, Paris.

'Augustus and his wife Livia never had any children together. Yet she is frequently depicted throughout the empire as being fertile – because these images aren't to do with her fertility or her sexuality, but to do with the fertility of the empire at large, the fertility brought about by the emperor. He brought the end of the civil wars; he brought peace and prosperity to the empire. And they are a celebration of that form of fertility. Therefore even though we know the names of these women, these carvings tells us very little about the women themselves. But it does show an emperor who can control his household, and an emperor who can control these women can certainly control an empire.

Roman texts of the time also stressed that perhaps people were not getting married as frequently as they should; perhaps they were not having children as often as they should and there are worries being expressed about the purity of the Roman race. All of this might be a response to social change. We don't know what actually was occurring, if there were fewer children, or fewer marriages, but we do know that one of Augustus' key aims was to be seen to be promoting the old traditional values. So he passed a series of laws to do with marriage and also adultery. In the marriage laws he was trying to encourage people to get married, but also they had to marry the right people. So he decreed which social classes could marry. He also set penalties for those who remained childless, or who didn't marry, and gave encouragement to those who did have children.'

The attempts made by Augustus to promote traditional family values were severely undermined by the disgraceful conduct of the only daughter of his previous marriage. By the time this great monument was being carved, Julia was already causing quite a stir, and the outrageous parties which were held at her home became the centre of Roman gossip. When the news of her adultery finally reached her father and stepmother Livia, they sternly reprimanded her. But she had borne her rather dull husband five children who seemed to resemble him, so perhaps things weren't all that bad. Julia, with typically scabrous wit, explained her flawless record by saying, 'I take on passengers ... only when the boat is full.' When her husband died in 12 BC, Julia became a merry widow at the age of 27, and her behaviour worsened. Even her new husband, the future Emperor Tiberius, fled to a faraway Greek island to avoid having to deal with her.

The Roman writer Seneca recorded the story:

'Augustus learned that she had been accessible to scores of lovers, that she had roamed the city in nocturnal revels, and that even the very steps in the Forum from which her father had proposed the laws against adultery had been chosen by his daughter for her debauched lovemaking. She had even sold her favours and sought every indulgence with unknown lovers as a prostitute.'

The distraught emperor first wrote a letter to the senate detailing his daughter's crimes, and then exiled her to the small barren island of Pandateria. Later he relented a little and moved her to Reggio di Calabria, where she died eleven years later in AD 14, in the same year as her father.

Ovid's Art of Love

The poet Ovid (Publius Ovidius Naso, 43 BC–AD 18), was punished by Augustus when he became involved in a scandal connected with the emperor's grand-daughter Julia, who was named after her mother and almost as debauched as she was. Ovid was banished to Tomi, a nasty little barbarian town on the Black Sea, and he never returned to Rome. Among his many works is the Ars Amatoria, *The Art of Love*, which is a typical handbook on seduction. This was completely

LEFT: Statue of a Roman matron, with elaborate coiffure, who is depicted as possibly giving an offering to the gods. 1st century BC. Archaeological Museum Naples.

ABOVE: The Capitoline Venus from behind. Also known as the 'callipygous Venus' which comes from the Greek meaning 'beautifully shaped buttocks', which this superb Roman sculpturing in marble clearly shows. Capitoline Museum, Rome.

OPPOSITE: From the front the Capitoline Venus modestly shields herself with both hands showing the full sensuality of the Roman goddess of love. Roman copy of an earlier Greek statue. 2nd century BC. Capitoline Museum, Rome.

at odds with the new morality enshrined in the emperor's laws. The precise nature of Ovid's offence is unknown, but even he admits it had something to do with Julia and his book, in which he wrote the following advice:

'The first thing to get into your head is that every single girl can be caught and that you'll catch her if you set your toils right. Birds will sooner fall dumb in springtime, cicadas stop in summer, or a hunting dog turn its back on a hare, than a lover's bland inducements can fail with a woman.'

He describes the way women should look and dress, and the type of coiffure that would be most attractive to men. But his advice did not stop there.

> Love's climax never should be rushed, I say,
> But worked up softly, lingering all the way.
> The parts a woman loves to have caressed
> Once found, caress, though modesty protest.

Ovid shows us the darker side of love, where lust meets brutality. In the circus, the gladiators might fight each other to the death, while condemned criminals or Christian martyrs might be torn apart by wild animals; the fashionable men and women of Rome, however, would watch their agonies unmoved, safe as they felt themselves to be from every attack except, from time to time, the stab of Cupid's arrow.

> Love oft in that arena fights a bout,
> Then 'tis the looker-on who's counted out.
> While chatting, buying a programme, shaking hands,
> Or wagering on the match, intent he stands,
> He feels the dart, and groaning 'neath the blow
> Himself becomes an item in the show.

Professor William Fitzgerald describes the gladiators themselves:

'They were both the dregs of society, and the rock stars of the ancient world. A graffito in Pompeii in the gladiatorial barracks claims that one of the gladiators is the heart-throb of the girls. We also read in Juvenal, the satirist, about a rich upper-class woman who chases around after a gladiator. In the ruins of Pompeii, after they had

dug away the pumice they discovered a series of crude sleeping rooms which turned out to be to be a gladiators' dormitory. There, frozen in time, was a gladiator who was holding in his arms, and no doubt protecting her from the hot ashes, an upper-class woman still wearing her jewels.

In Ovid's day violence and bloodshed were the principal attractions for circus audiences; some years after his death, however, and particularly with the building of the Colosseum, sex began to play an increasingly important part in the entertainment, with re-enactments of mythical couplings between beasts and humans. The one between Parsiphae and the bull must have been fatal and was probably staged as an execution.

Ovid's image of the ideal but slightly protesting woman is summed up by the statue of the Capitoline Venus whose attitude, with her hand across her breast, suggests that she is trying both to hide herself and to offer herself simultaneously. Her soft, sensuous body is a little heavier than the modern ideal, but looking behind the statue it is clear how she got her name 'the Callipygian

OPPOSITE: Mars (or Ares), the god of war, not fighting but relaxed and in love. This statue is known as the 'Ares Ludovisi' and is possibly from the Temple of Mars in Rome. Also it could have been sculpted by Skopas Minor in the late 2nd century BC, or be a Roman copy of 2nd century AD. Palazzo Altemps Museum, Rome.

LEFT: The little Cupid looking up at Mars from under his right leg. This charming touch was added when the statue was restored by Gian Lorenzo Bernini in about 1620 AD. The original could have been sculpted by Skopas Minor in the late 2nd century BC, or be a Roman copy of 2nd century AD. Palazzo Altemps Museum, Rome.

RIGHT: Terracotta relief of a *bestiarius* gladiator
(animal fighter). As the fragment shown here is
made from a mould, a complete cast of this
terracotta scene, discovered too late to include, is
at the Archaeological Museum in Naples
and shows that the gladiator is looking to his
left because a lion is about to pounce. 1st
century AD. British Museum, London.

ABOVE: Terracotta group of two gladiators
fighting, with shields and swords. Gladiators
were usually criminals. 1st century AD. British
Museum, London.

OPPOSITE: This amphitheatre in Pompeii is
the oldest known one in Italy, built the year
Pompeii became a Roman colony in 80 BC.
It could hold 20,000 people, and measures
135 x 104 metres. 80 BC. Pompeii, Italy.

behind makes her a sculpture in the round indeed, the epitome of Roman
sensuality.

Male statuary, too, reveals the same softer, more sensual approach; this
portrayal of Mars, lover of Venus and god of war, is a case in point. Unlike Ares,
his Greek counterpart, who would have been represented standing poised for the
fray, this Roman statue adopts the body language of love – he is sitting down,
his muscles relaxed, staring thoughtfully ahead. We know that he is in love
because he has a little Cupid, with his bow, sitting on the floor and looking
smilingly up at him. Although the figure of Cupid, together with the hilt
of the god's sword and one or two other details, were restored in the seventeenth
century by Gianlorenzo Bernini, the composition itself remains unaltered.

Sex and violence were as closely connected in the ancient world as they
are in the world of today. After Ovid's death the great Colosseum was built,
which brought these two elements to a nadir of depravity. The insatiable public
was able to see not only killings, but re-enactments of mythical couplings
between beasts and humans. The one of 'Pasiphae and the Bull', in which the
bull was lowered in a cage and harness on to the poor female victim, may have
been a type of execution. It was certainly depraved.

12 *The Beginning of the End*

BELOW: Agrippina, mother of the Emperor
Nero. She married three times: Nero was
from her first marriage. Her third husband
was her uncle the Emperor Claudius. *c.* 55 AD.
Archaeological Museum, Naples.
OPPOSITE: Arch of Hadrian in Athens, made
of Pentelic marble, erected by Emperor
Hadrian. The gateway is 18 metres high and
12.5 metres wide. 132 AD. South of the
Zappeion Gardens, Athens.

The destruction of Pompeii by the eruption of Vesuvius in 79 symbolized the end of a notably decadent period for Rome under the last of the line of the Caesars, the infamous Emperor Nero.

Nero was a grotesque example of Lord Acton's dictum, 'Power tends to corrupt; absolute power corrupts absolutely.' Right from the start, the gods were against him. His father Domitian died when he was three, and his mother Agrippina was banished soon afterwards. He was brought up by an aunt, under the care of a dancer and a barber who were his two slave 'tutors' – hardly an ideal start to the life of an emperor. Later the Stoic philosopher Seneca was put in charge of his education, and is supposed to have encouraged his first love affairs with boys. In 54 AD, at the age of 16, he became Emperor, and in the same year he seduced and subsequently poisoned Britannicus, the 14-year-old son of his debauched stepmother Messalina.

By the time he was twenty, Nero had both a wife, Octavia, and a powerful and beautiful mistress, Poppaea. Together, the two women plotted to murder his mother Agrippina, who had already tried to seduce her son. They invited her to the popular resort of Baiae, where well-to-do Romans came to take the waters, bathe in the natural hot springs and build themselves sumptuous holiday villas. The plan was to send Agrippina out to sea in a boat equipped with a special device which, at a given moment, would cause it automatically to spring a leak and sink, leaving her to be drowned. On the chosen day, however, the sea was dead calm and the device failed to work. Knowing now that her son was

ABOVE: Roman mosaic floor in terraced remains of the vast thermal complex at Baiae, over the gulf of Pozzuoli. The largest thermal centre of ancient Italy, Caesar, Cicero, Pompey and others all had their sea-side villas at Baiae. 1st century BC. Baiae, near Naples, Italy.

OPPOSITE: The Thermal Bath complex at Baiae. There were four main 'thermae, called erroneously the Temples of Diana, Mercury, Venus and Sosandra. In fact they were all domed roofed baths, the oldest and best preserved of which was Mercury, the dome of which can be seen on p. 155.

trying to murder her, she fled to her own villa nearby; but no sooner had she arrived than Nero sent a party of soldiers who clubbed her and stabbed her to death.

Nero's next move was to exile his wife Octavia to the Pandateria, the same island to which Augustus had sent his daughter, the erring Julia, years before. On arrival there, she was immediately executed on a charge of treason. He was now free to raise his mistress Poppaea to the throne, but she too was doomed. One day, when she was rash enough to reprove him for returning late from the races, he lost his temper and kicked her to death. His monstrous behaviour continued unchecked; literally dozens of senators, generals and noblemen were assassinated on his orders, often for no better reason than that he was jealous of their ability or success. Even his old tutor, Seneca, was forced to commit suicide.

Nero is perhaps best known mainly for his persecution of the small Christian community in Rome, which he held responsible for the fire that devastated the city

RIGHT: The Charioteer, an imposing bronze of the 'severe style' who holds only the reins of the four missing horses. He wears a long pleated *chiton* which has a high belt and straps at the back to prevent it from fluttering and distracting the horses. According to an inscription the group was given to the temple of Apollo at Delphi by Polyzalus of Gela in Italy in gratitude for winning the races at the Pythian Games (Games held in the stadium at Delphi) in *c.* 478 BC. Bronze. Museum at Delphi, Greece.

BELOW: Bust of Hadrian as the new Emperor. 2nd century AD. Archaeological Museum, Naples.

in 64 AD. In fact he had almost certainly started it himself to clear the land for an enormous new palace he was planning to build. By this time, however, he was so hated in Rome that he had begun to fear seriously for his life. He fled to Greece, but here too he quickly antagonized his local subjects. They were particularly insulted when he tried to reschedule the sacred Olympic Games to fit in with his travel plans, adding singing and lyre-playing to the events which, although they were part of the Olympic ceremony, were not an actual event in order that he could enter – and inevitably win – the contests himself.

Returning to Rome in 68 AD, Nero entered the city at the head of a huge triumphal procession, his Olympic Prizes being carried aloft before him. To the army, this was an insult; to the populace it merely rendered him more ridiculous. Soon there was a revolt in Spain, where the legions acclaimed the local governor, Galba, as the new Emperor. Nero fled in panic to a slaves' estate in the suburbs of Rome, from which he hoped to escape to Greece; but when he heard that the Senate had rallied to Galba and that the Praetorian Guard was already on its way to arrest him, he ordered his secretary to cut his throat.

With Nero safely in his grave, what was left of Rome slowly began to recover from his reign of terror. There followed, however, another year of uncertainty during which Galba made himself unpopular in his turn and was duly assassinated by the Praetorian Guard. Six more relatively undistinguished Emperors followed in swift succession until eventually, in 98 AD, there came one of the greatest – Trajan – under whom the Roman Empire achieved its greatest extent. He died in 117 and was succeeded by his ward Hadrian, the son of an upper-class Roman family long resident in Spain.

The Emperor and the Young Adonis

Hadrian had married Sabina, Trajan's great-niece, when she was fourteen years old – an arranged marriage which had greatly strengthened his claim to the succession. (The Roman Empire was not – at least in

LEFT: Sabina and her husband Hadrian as Venus and Mars, which is supposed to show that they were as in love as the gods they represented in marble. Sabina is gazing up at her husband with arms outstretched, while Hadrian looks thoughtfully into the middle distance. 2nd century AD. Ref: Ma 1009. Louvre Museum, Paris.

theory – hereditary, passing automatically from father to son, although in practice it often did so.) Since Emperors were inevitably idealized – and later deified – it comes as no surprise to find a sculpted group portraying Sabina and a naked Hadrian as that famous pair of lovers from the Roman pantheon, Venus and Mars. In fact, however, the Emperor was – like Trajan before him – predominantly homosexual, his constant travels being probably due as much to psychological and sexual restlessness as to the necessity of inspecting the boundaries of the Empire, which was by then seriously overstretched.

In 128 Hadrian and Sabina arrived at Corinth. Among their entourage was a beautiful 18-year-old Greek boy named Antinous, who had been trained as an

LEFT: Bust of Antinous. 2nd century AD. Archaeological Museum, Naples.

BELOW: One of the best statues of Antinous, found still standing upright in Delphi in 1893. The curly hair is made of a different coloured marble and would have supported a golden wreath. With its melancholy expression and slightly downcast head, the statue says all it meant to be loved by and to have died for the most important man in the world at that time. Slightly larger than life-size. 130–138 AD. Delphi Museum, Greece.

imperial page in Rome. His good looks can still be seen in the countless statues of him which were made at Hadrian's command. Hadrian himself, who spoke better Greek than Latin, would always have seen himself as the erastes, or loving tutor, and Antinous as his eromenos, the loving and beloved pupil, a relationship which demonstrated as clearly as anything could, the continued hold of the old Greek influences on the Roman world.

One of the purposes of Hadrian's visit to Greece was to witness the secret religious rituals of the Eleusis – they were known as the Eleusian mysteries, and remain mysterious to us even today – and to consult the oracles, the most famous of which was at Delphi, which had already been in existence for over a thousand years. An exquisite marble statue of Antinous was discovered there as recently as 1893, still standing upright. Later Christians, disgusted by a relationship which would have seemed perfectly acceptble to the vast majority of the Emperor's subjects, tried to blacken the young man's character; but one of the few contemporary descriptions of him praises his intelligence and wisdom and speaks of 'strength of mind and understanding'.

While he was in Athens Hadrian had the idea of making it the new capital of his Empire. He initiated the building of an immense temple to Zeus-Jupiter and declared himself a god, accepting the title of Olympius from the grateful Athenians. Hadrian and his whole entourage settled down to spend another six months in Athens. He and Antinous actually spent the next six months in the city – for him an almost unprecedented length of stay in one place – passing much of their time in the study of philosophy and of the Eleusian mysteries that had so profoundly affected

ABOVE: Temple to Olympian Zeus. The largest temple in Greece, it took 700 years to build and was completed in honour of Hadrian's arrival in Athens in 130 AD. Originally there were 104 Corinthian columns in Pentelic marble of which only 15 are now standing. Hadrian put up a vast statue to Zeus and a huge one of himself inside the temple. 108 x 41 metres. 500 BC–130 AD. Athens.

them. In Athens too – where St Paul had preached half a century earlier – the Emperor is said to have studied for the first time the doctrines of Christianity. He stopped the persecution of the Christians in Athens; apart from that, however, he does not seem to have been particularly impressed – the new religion certainly did nothing to soften his attitude towards Palestine, where the Jews had launched a major rebellion against Rome in 70 AD (eventually put down only after a major expedition by the Emperor Titus) and were still causing trouble.

But the Emperor's wanderlust never left him for long. June 129 found him in Syria, but here his visit seemed fated from the start. When he and Antinous climbed to the top of Mount Casius to make a dawn sacrifice to Zeus, both the sacrificial animal and the priest were killed by a sudden thunderbolt – an omen which seemed so unfavourable that they left hurriedly for Jerusalem. Hadrian reached the holy city in a dangerous mood. Despite his studies in Athens he continued to mistrust both the Jewish and the Christian religions, which he saw as threats to the Graeco-Roman civilization for which he stood. Unable to stamp them out, he nevertheless forbade the Jewish practice of circumcision and ordered the building of another temple to Zeus on the site of Solomon's Temple, the most sacred site in all Jerusalem. Then, having renamed the city Aelia Capitolina, he left – wisely, for he was now so unpopular there that he might easily have been assassinated – for Egypt.

Egypt and the Nile

Hadrian arrived in Alexandria – the richest city in the Empire in August 130, to find that his reputation had preceded him. The city was full of troublemakers and it was largely to escape the intensely hostile atmosphere that he organized the famous expedition to hunt a huge man-eating lion that was terrorizing the local populations. When they eventually tracked it down the Emperor wounded it with a well-thrown spear, but the furious animal then charged straight at Antinous, who would certainly have been killed had not Hadrian hurled a second spear just in time. He returned to Alexandria in triumph and ordered medals to be struck

BELOW: Ruins of part of Hadrian's Villa – the Great Baths – in the sunset. The gigantic villa, covering nearly 300 acres near Tivoli, an area about one hour east of Rome, had many different architectural styles as reminders to Hadrian of his visits throughout the Empire. There was also a huge network of underground passages, so servants and services could move around the villa without disturbing the upper level. Building took from 118–133 AD.

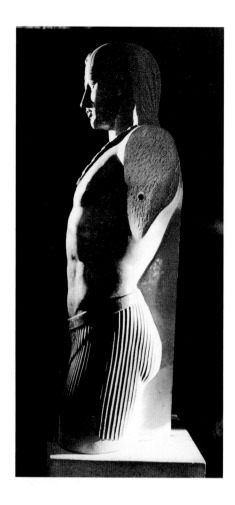

commemorating the victory of the god-Emperor over the king of beasts.

Next on the imperial itinerary was a journey up the Nile, where the annual flood had failed for the second year in succession – another sure sign, in the eyes of the Egyptians, that the gods were angry. Hadrian consulted the priests and astrologers, and cannot have been altogether pleased to learn that in times past the pharaoh himself had been sacrificed, or had sacrificed his daughter, to appease the god of the great river. He then left, with a fleet of barges, for the city of Thebes, stopping at Memphis to visit the sanctuary of Apis, the sacred bull.

Half-way to Thebes the boats stopped at a local shrine, where yet again the Emperor consulted the local priests and was told the story of Isidora, a local girl of fifteen who had just drowned in the Nile. Because the river was known to grant eternal life to all those who perished in it, she was already the centre of a local cult. Continuing still further upstream, the fleet passed a small temple to the Ramesses II near the little mud-built village of Hir-wer; and it was here that Antinous mysteriously disappeared.

On his return to Rome, the devastated Hadrian could only repeat the words, 'He fell into the Nile'. Then he returned to his magnificent villa at Tivoli outside the city – the remains of which can still be visited today – to mourn the death of the one human being he had loved above all others. There too, before he died, he was to build a vast Graeco-Egyptian memorial, identifying Antinous with both Dionysus and Osiris. The beautiful boy, he felt, must have been a god; and, without consulting the Senate, he ordered a cult to be established to worship this new divinity. Games were held for centuries thereafter in the boy's honour, statues of him were turned

ABOVE: Profile of Antinous as an Egyptian god, probably Osiris. On 30 October 130 AD, the day of Antinous' death, Hadrian founded a huge city in northern Egypt – Antinoupolis. 2nd century AD. Height 1.35 metres. Ref: WAF 24. Egyptian Museum, Munich.

RIGHT: A stone crocodile near the waters of the Canopus canal in Hadrian's villa. The Canopus reproduced the Egyptian temple of Serapis on the canal to Alexandria. Building took from 118–133 AD. Hadrian's villa, Tivoli.

OPPOSITE: Arched colonnade at western end of the Canopus. There were also many copies of famous Greek sculptures around the long pool, including four copies of the caryatids from the Erechtheum from Athens. Many statues of Antinous were found in this area, and some feel he is buried in here. Hadrian's villa, Tivoli.

out by the hundred, and a huge obelisk was erected in Rome itself. Antinous was the last non-imperial mortal to be so deified, just as his was the only non-imperial head to appear on the royal coinage.

In 136 AD Hadrian suffered one of his frequent haemorrhages, more serious than any of its predecessors. He recovered, but saw that the time had come for him – since he and Sabina were childless – to pick a successor. His first choice fell on a certain Lucius Commodus, a 35-year-old aristocrat whose chief claims to fame were his looks and the invention of a meat pie of which the Emperor was particularly fond; but he too was a sick man who, feeling in need of a pick-me-up before making his first speech to the Senate, took too much of the prescribed medicine and died of an overdose. He was followed to the grave shortly afterwards by Sabina herself. Hadrian had never liked her much: he granted her the divine status that was her due and mourned her as tradition demanded, but otherwise had her buried with the minimum of ceremony. Meanwhile his thoughts turned again to the question of his

OPPOSITE: One of a pair of magnificent marble Centaurs which were found in Hadrian's villa. The baroque carving is a superb imitation of bronze made in black marble signed by two sculptors from Aphrodisias. 2nd century AD. Capitoline Museum, Rome.

ABOVE: The Maritime Theatre, Hadrian's Villa. This was a place to which Hadrian liked to escape the world; and once across the circular canal there was a small villa on the central island into which he could retire and hide. 118–133 AD. Hadrian's villa, Tivoli.

ABOVE: Relief showing the Apotheosis of Sabina, with Hadrian watching seated below. Sabina is at the extreme top of the sculpture above the winged deity, while a young man (Antinous?) gesticulates to Hadrian. 2nd century AD. Conservatori Museum, Rome.

successor. This time he selected a conservative senator by the name of Antoninus Pius – and none too soon, for he himself was by now seriously ill. In his depression he attempted suicide, but his doctor took away the poison (and, we are told, drank it instead). Next he tried to stab himself, but the dagger was snatched from him. Finally he retired with his court to Baiae, where, in defiance of medical orders, he deliberately drank himself to death. He died on 10 July 138 AD.

Although the hieroglyphs on Antinous' obelisk suggest that his mummified body still lies somewhere in the grounds of Hadrian's villa, the mystery of his death remains unresolved. It may – as the Emperor himself suggested – have been an accident. Or it may have been suicide – the suicide of a young man who has outgrown his beautiful boyhood and feels unable to continue in his role as the eromenos of his god-emperor. It may even have been a sacrifice according to the wishes of the ancient Egyptian priests, intended to appease the god of the Nile and thereby to safeguard the imperial prestige. Would Hadrian have ever willingly offered up the love of his life? Or did Antinous drown himself on his own initiative? We shall never know. 'He fell into the Nile': we must leave it at that.

Antinous – Adonis – Adonai

Antinous was not just the fantasy of a megalomaniac. He was a symbol of both the Greek civilization that was fading fast and of the yearning for new – and more satisfactory – religious beliefs. He struck the balance between the classical religions of Egypt, Greece and Rome, and the eastern concept of salvation through death. In a way he was Adonis, the young demigod who died in his prime, whom all could love and for whom all could weep; and he was Adonai, the young Hebrew 'lord' who was

LEFT: Togate statue of Hadrian, in the role as Chief Priest. His face sculpted here shows his sadness at this stage in his life. 2nd century AD. Capitoline Museum, Rome.

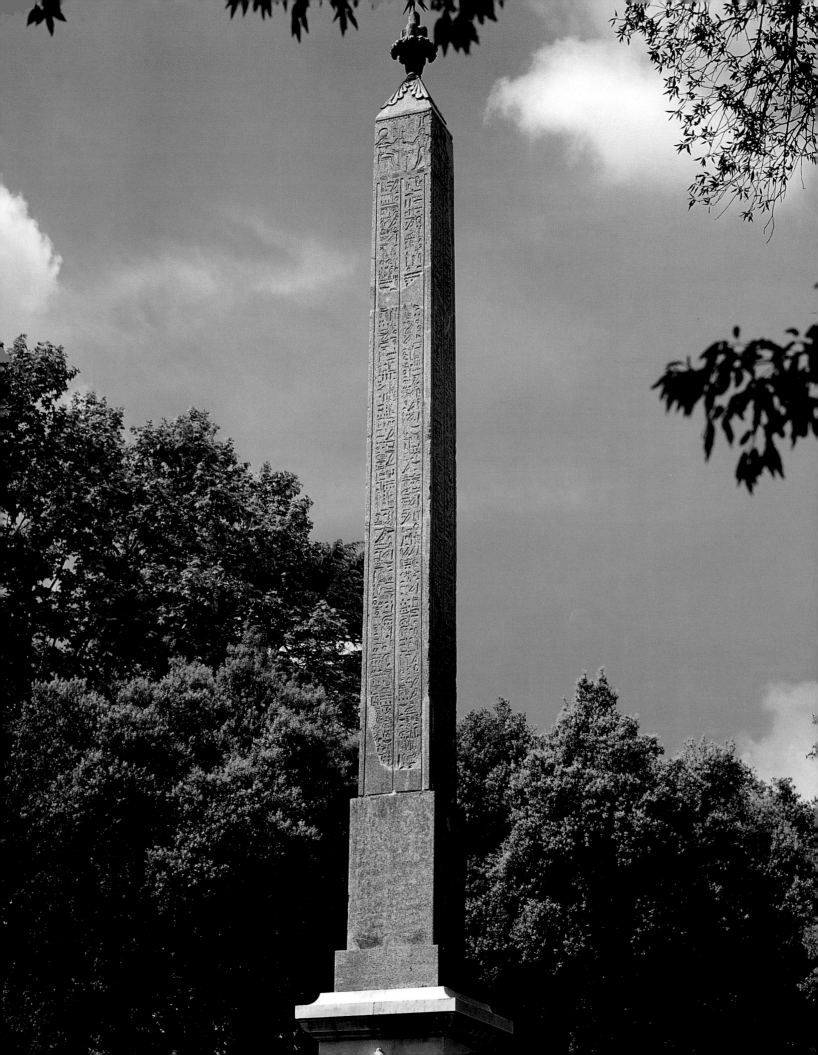

sacrificed for a cause. No wonder the early Christians feared his popularity and power, bitterly resenting both his deification and the festivals which continued for hundreds of years after his death. Thousands of statues were made in Antinous' honour, and over 120 authenticated statues or busts exist in museums throughout the world which were made during the second century AD. When Lord Tennyson stopped in front of one in the British Museum he said, 'Ah! the inscrutable Bithynian! If we knew what *he* knew we should understand the ancient world.'

Hadrian also constructed an obelisk to him, which has now been erected on the Pincio hill in Rome, but no one knows where Antinous is buried. However, a recent reading of the hieroglyphs seems to give some indication of this: 'O, Antinous! this deceased one, who rests in this tomb in the country estate of the Emperor of Rome.' Excavations carried out since in Hadrian's villa have revealed nothing of Antinous' grave, but four caryatids and two enormous Sileni were found in the Canopus canal in 1952, which as mythological beings often used to bear canopies over graves. Maybe the secret of Antinous's grave and the real reason why he died

OPPOSITE: The Obelisk to Antinous on the Pincio Hill in Rome. Where it stood in antiquity is not known. The illustration above shows the top of the obelisk. Rome, Italy.

169

ABOVE: Aphrodite fighting off the attentions of Pan (see p. 62) with her son Eros fluttering beside his mother. In Christian paintings, putti and angels replaced the flying Erotes. National Archaeological Museum, Athens.

OPPOSITE: The Temple of Isis at Delos. A simple and imposing Doric temple, repaired by the Athenians in 135 BC, shows how far her cult had come from Egypt. Much later, the pagan statue of Isis with her child Horus was sometimes transformed into the Virgin Mary holding the infant Jesus. The temple stands, like many a classical Christian church, with the statue of its goddess inside. Delos, Greece.

will never be known. So let Hadrian have the last words through the hieroglyphs on the obelisk: 'Osiris Antinous, the just, grew to a youth with a beautiful countenance, on whom the eyes rejoiced...'

Near where Hadrian died, in her cave in the mountain lived the strange prophetess, the Sibyl of Cumae. She had already prophesied in words that no Roman then understood: 'He will satisfy five thousand from five loaves and a fish of the sea.' The Sibyl also prophesied: 'Jesus Christ shall come from heaven, and live and reign in poverty on earth.'

After Hadrian Rome began its long decline; and less than two centuries after his death the Emperor Constantine the Great was to declare the doctrine of which he had thought so little to be the official religion of the empire. The long line of female divinities who had received the adoration of the ancient world, from the earliest Earth-Mother through the goddesses of Mesopotamia and Egypt, Greece and Rome, now yielded in their turn to a new and far greater successor, from whom was to spring the long-awaited Adonai: Mary the Theotokos, Mother of God.

ΝΑΟΣ ΤΗΣ ΙΣΙΔΟΣ
TEMPLE D'ISIS

Bibliography

Amour des Dieux et des Hommes, 1989. *Eros Greek*, Ministere de la Culture de Grece: Athens.

Andronicos, M. 1984. *Vergina*: Athens.

Ascherson, N. 1957. *A Traveller in Rome*: London

Ascherson, N. 1969. *A Traveller in Southern Italy*: London

Ascherson, N. 1995. *Black Sea*: London

Bachofen, J. J. 1967. *Myth, Religion, and Mother Right: Selected Writings of J. J. Bachofen.* Trans. R. Manheim: London.

Barber, R. 1987. *Greece Blue Guide*: London.

Baring, A. & Cashford, J. 1991. *The Myth of the Goddess: Evolution of an Image*: London.

Bonfante, L. 1973. 'Etruscan Women: A Question of Interpretation', in *Archaeology* 26, 242–9.

Bonfante, L. 1981. 'Etruscan Couples and their Aristocratic Society,' in Foley, H. P. ed. *Reflections of Women in Antiquity*, 323–42: New York, London, Paris.

Bonfante, L. 1982. 'Subject Matter in the Engravings and Reliefs on Etruscan Mirrors: Daily Life', in Thomson de Grummond, N. ed. *A Guide to Etruscan Mirrors*. Ch. VII: Talahassee, Florida.

Bonfante, L. 1984. 'The Women of Etruria', in Peradotto, J. and Sullivan, J. P. eds. *Women in the Ancient World: The Arethusa Papers*: New York.

Bonfante, L. 1986. 'Daily Life and Afterlife', in Bonfante, L. ed. *Etruscan Life and Afterlife*, 232–78: Warminster.

Bonfante, L. 1990. *Etruscan*: London.

Cantarella, E. 1987. *Pandora's Daughters: The Role and Status of Women in Greek and Roman Antiquity*: Baltimore.

Carpiceci, A. C. & Pennino, L. 1995. *Paestum and Velia*: Italy.

Davrill, T. 1987. *Prehistoric Britain*: London.

Delporte, H. 1993. 'Gravettian Female Figurines: A Regional Survey', in Knecht, H. Pike-Tay, A. & White, R. eds. *Before Lascaux: The Complex Record of the Early Upper Paleolithic*: Boca Raton.

Dyer, J. 1981. *The Penguin Guide to Prehistoric England and Wales*: London.

Ehrenberg, M. 1989. *Women in Prehistory*: London.

Eisler, R. 1995. *Sacred Pleasure*: New York.

Fitts, D. 1962. *Lysistrata of Aristophanes*: London.

Flaceliere, R. 1962. *Love In Ancient Greece*: London.

Freeman, C. 1996. *Egypt, Greece and Rome*: New York.

Gimbutas, M. 1979/1982. *The Goddesses and Gods of Old Europe: 6500–3500 B.C. Myths and Cult Images*: London.

Grane, R. 1955. *Greek Myths 1 & 2*: London.

Graves, R. 1984. *Greek Myths*: London.

Green, P. 1990. *Alexander to Aetium*: London.

Greer, G. 1995. *Slip-Shod Sibyls*: London

Griffiths, R. J. 1990. *Paestum: Greeks and Romans in Southern Italy*: London.

Grigson, G. 1970. *The Goddess of Love*: London.

Heurgon, J. 1964. *Daily Life of the Etruscans.* Trans. Kirkup, J.: London.

Holloway, R. R. 1986. 'The Bulls in the "Tomb of the Bulls" at Tarquinia', in *AJA* 90, 447–52.

Hughs-Hallett, L. 1990. *Cleopatra – Histories, Dreams and Distortions*: London

James, E. O. 1959. *The Cult of the Mother–Goddess: An Archaeological and Documentary Study*: London.

Johns, C. 1982. *Sex or Symbol: Erotic Images of Greece and Rome*: London.

Keuls, E. C. 1993. *The Reign of the Phallus*: Berkeley, Los Angeles and London.

Kiefe, O. 1990. *Sexual Life in Ancient Rome*: London.

Kilmer, M. 1993. *Greek Erotica on Attic Red-Figure Vases*: London

Lambert, L. & Thomson de Grummond, N. 1982. 'The Usage of Etruscan Mirrors', in Thomson de Grummond, N. ed. *A Guide to Etruscan Mirrors*. Ch. IX: Talahassee.

Lambert, R. 1984. *Beloved and God*: London.

Levick, B. 1976. 'The Fall of Julia the Younger', in *Latomus* (35), 301–39.

Macnamara, E. 1973. *Everyday Life of the Etruscans*: London.

Manniche, L. 1983. *Sexual Life in Ancient Egypt*: London.

Montserrat, D. 1996. *Sex and Society in Graeco-Roman Egypt*: London.

Norwood, F. 1963. 'The Riddle of Ovid's *Relegatio,*' in *Classical Philology* (58), 150–63.

Nugent, S. G. 1990. '*Tristia* 2: Ovid and Augustus', in Raaflaub, Kurt A. and Toher, Mark, eds. *Between Republic and Empire: Interpretations of Augustus and his Principate*, 239–257: Berkeley, Los Angeles and London.

Pallottino, M. 1975. *The Etruscans.* Trans. Cremona, J.: London.

Raaflaub, K. A. & Samons, L. J. 'Opposition to Augustus', in Raaflaub, Kurt A. & Toher, Mark eds. *Between Republic and Empire: Interpretations of Augustus and his Principate*, 417–54: Berkeley, Los Angeles and London.

Radice, B. 1973. *Who's Who in the Ancient World*: London.

Reeder, E.D. 1995. *Pandora*: Baltimore.

Richmond, I. 1969. *Roman Archaeology and Art*, Salway, Peter, ed.: London.

'sardi'. 1992. *Erotic Love Through the Ages*: New York.

Scullard, H.H. 1976. *From the Gracchi to Nero: A History of Rome from 133 B.C. to A.D. 68*: London.

Seton-Williams, V. and Stocks, P. 1993. *Egypt Blue Guide*: London.

Sieveking, A. 1979. *The Cave Artists*: London

Spivey, N. and Stoddart, S. 1990. *Etruscan Italy*: Italy

Steingraber, S. ed. 1986. *Etruscan Painting.* Eng. version ed. D. & F. R. Ridgeway, trans. M. Blair: New York.

Syme, R. 1939. *The Roman Revolution*: Oxford.

Syme, R. 1978. *History in Ovid*: Oxford.

Tannahill, R. 1980. *Sex in History*: London.

Taphin, O. 1989. *Greek Fire*: London.

Taylor, T. 1996. *The Prehistory of Sex*: London.

The Atlas of Archaeology, 1987: London.

Themelis, P.G. 1980. *Delphi*: Athens.

Velikovsky, I. 1960. *Oedipus and Akhnaton*: London.

Ward-Perkins, J. and Claridge, A. 1976. *Pompeii AD 79*: Boston.

Warner, M. 1994. *From the Beast to the Blonde*: London.

Waterfield, R. 1996. *Plato Symposium*: New York.

Wilkinson, L.P. 1962. *Ovid Surveyed*: Cambridge.

Willets, R.F. 1969. *Everyday Life in Ancient Crete*: London.

Winkler, J. 1990. *The Constraints of Desire*: New York.

Zacks, R. 1994. *History Laid Bare*: London.

Zaphiroponlon, P. 1993. *Delos*: Athens.

Acknowledgements

This book is dedicated to the memory of Professor Kenan Erim

This book is dedicated to a dear friend and a great archaeologist, the late Kenan Erim, who sadly died in 1990, but in the summer of 1984, as the then Director of Excavations of Aphrodisias, he brought myself and John Julius Norwich together to work on a film in that remarkable city in western Turkey.

John Julius' sheer professionalism and knowledge of Hellenistic architecture saved the first day of shooting and began a lasting friendship, so I am very grateful for all the encouragement and help he has given me during the making of our next film together 'Love in the Ancient World' and this new book. Many other friendships were also made in Aphrodisias, and some of the archaeologists, whom I met around Kenan's lively dinner table at the site, have kindly offered their help and advice. Among them were Juliette de La Genière, Nathalie de Chaisemartin, Charlotte Roueche and Joyce Reynolds the epigraphist, who introduced me to a young man wanting to get into films, Thomas Fegan, who became an invaluable researcher and assistant throughout the filming.

At Aphrodisias I also met the sculptor/restorer Peter Rockwell, whose knowledge of Greek and Roman sculpture has added a deeper meaning to the story behind those ancient chisel blows. Other invaluable contributors without whom this book would not exist include – Dr Paul Bahn, Anne Baring, Dr Dominic Montserrat, Professor Eva Keuls, Dr Wuenscher, Dr Ellen Reeder, Professor Theo Antikas, Dr William Fitzgerald, Dr Susan Fischler and Dr Mary Beard.

Most of the photographs and research were only possible because of the film, so my thanks to Richard Price of Primetime Associates, who started the project with me and saw it through with the Arts and Entertainment Television Network in New York. Thanks also to Marina Gratsos and Felix von Moreau, who not only got the very patient Dr Walter Flemmer of Bayerische Rundfunk involved, but they also helped in every way possible throughout the year with our production manager Ulla Streib. The Ancient World is nothing much without Greece and the help given by George Culucundis and ERT AE Television was invaluble; also much of my photography would not have been possible without the lighting of my cameraman, Alistair Cameron, and his talented and helpful crew.

There are also those people who gave me generous hospitality before and during the film: the late Joan and Seymour Camrose on whose yacht the idea was dreamed up, Tricia and Timothy Daunt and Bert Smith, the present Aphrodisias site director, in Turkey; Sam and Rosetta Miller in New York; and Monica von Moreau in Germany. In England the help given by Ingrid McAlpine, Peter Watts and his son Mark also gave me the encouragement needed to continue.

Anyone who knows the problems that plague a film-maker will know that they manage to quadruple if you try to write a book at the same time, so I appreciated all the effort Michael Dover, Judith Flanders and Caroline Knight made in hauling me away from the editing table to produce texts and photographs.

Finally only someone special would have put up with a drawing-room and a study littered for weeks on end with large reference books and piles of photographs, together with cans of film and video tapes, with the occasional visits and feeding of actors and film crews, let alone the painting of the film set – the goddess of love herself (and her daughter) – my long suffering wife Suzy and daughter Sophie.

CHRISTOPHER MILES 12 JUNE 1997
CALSTONE HOUSE, WILTSHIRE.

All photographs taken by Christopher Miles other than those listed below:
p. 6 John Reader, Archive Science Museum; pp. 13, 16 Musée d'Aquitaine, France; p. 18 Dr Dimitri Chermisin; p. 26 Etching by Suzy Miles; p. 40 Egypt color; pp. 44, 47, 48 a, 49 l, John Decopoulos; 61, 62 b Gregory Dupré; 72 r John and Mable Ringling Museum of Art, USA; 95 Baltimore Museum of Art, Baltimore, USA; 110 Professor Harry T. Moore. The author would like to to thank: Gerald Pollinger of Laurence Pollinger for the estate of D. H. Lawrence, for permission to quote from *Etruscan Places* (in ch. 8); and the Penguin Group, for quotations from *The Love Songs of Sappho*, trans. Paul Roche, first published by Signet Classics, NY, July 1966 (in ch. 5), and Plato's *Symposium*, trans. Walter Hamilton, first published by Penguin Classics 1951 (in ch. 5).

Index

Figures in italics refer to captions.

Abraham 27, 29
Achelous *112*
Achilles 96, *113*
Acropolis 55, *56, 60, 63*
Actaeon 117
Actium, naval battle 139
Acton, Lord 152
Adam 27–8
Adonai festival 91–3, *93*, 104
Adonis *50*, 91–3, *93*, 167
Aebutius 128, 130
Aeetes 97
Aelia Capitolina 161
Aeschines 73–4
afterlife 35
agape 63
Agathon 56, 57, 63, 64, 65
agriculture 21, 22
Agrippa *143*
Agrippina, mother of Nero 152, *152*, 154
Ahken-aton *37*
Ahmosis, Queen 34–5
Akhenaten 37, *37*, 38
Alcibiades 57, 77, 85–6, 104, *104*, 105
Alexander the Great 68, 130, 133
Alexandria 138, 139, 161, *162*
    the Library of 139
    Pharos lighthouse 139
alphabet 52
Alta, Norway 17
Amanitou, Antigone *90*
Amazons 96, *96*
Amenhotep III, Pharaoh 37
Amun *33*, 34, 35, 37, *37, 42*
Amun-Re (supreme deity) 34
Anacreon 56
anal sex 63, 74, *75*
andron (men's quarters) *52*, 56
Antikas, Professor Theo 71
Antinoopolis *162*
Antinous 157, 159, *159*, 160, 161, 162, *162*, 165, 166–7, 169–70
Antiphon Painter *93*
Antony, Mark 138, *139*, 140
'Aphrodisian school' of sculptors *59*
Aphrodisias, Turkey *26, 59*, 140
Aphrodite 17, *17*, 26, *26, 50*, 58, 59, *59*, 60, *60*, 62, 63, *75*, 78, 79, *84*, 91, 92, 94, 118, 130, 140, *170*
Aphrodite of Knidos 75, 77
Apis (sacred bull) 162
Apollo *84*, 97, *99*, 118

Apollodorus *82*
Apuleius, Lucius *82*
Arcadia 99, *99*
Arch of Hardian, Athens *152*
Ares 92, 118, 149
'Ares Ludovisi' *149*
Ariadne 44, 47, *49*
Aristodemus 57
Aristogeiton 63
Aristogiton *63*
Aristophanes 57, 63, 64–5, 70, 79, 81, 88, 90, *90, 91*, 105
Aristotle 86
Ark of the Covenant 29
Ars Pacis (Altar of Peace) monument *140, 143*
The Art of Love (Ovid) 145–6
'art' object, world's first man-made 10–11
Artemis *99*, 117
artificial insemination *24*
Asklepios (god of healing) *44*
Aspasia *60*, 74–5
Assyrians 28
Aten (sun god) 37, *37*
Athena *56*, 118
Athens 51, 159–60
    Adonis and the festival for women 91–3
    homosexuality and the law of Athens 73–4
    men's fear of women in love 95–7
    the phallic symbol 97–102
    the rise of 52–60
    woman as vessel 93–4
    women, love and war 88–90
Atlas 97
Atum 30
Augustus, Emperor *140*, 143–4, 145, 154
Aurignacians 14
Ave, Avu (moon-queen) 21
Avebury stone circle and earth works 20, *21*

Bacchanalia 127–8, 130
Bahn, Dr Paul 10, 14, 15
Baiae, near Naples 135, 137, 152, *154*, 166
'Band of Thebes' 68
'Barberini' faun *102*
Baring, Anne 16
barren wives 24, *24*
Bath, Marquess of 21
Bath, Virginia, Marchioness of 21

bathroom, Palace of Nestor 48, *48*
Baudelaire, Charles 8
Beard, Dr Mary 123
Berekhat Ram, Israel 10
Bernini, Gian Lorenzo *149*, 150
Bernini, Giovanni Battista *81*
Bogazkoy, Anatolia 26
Bonfante 117
Book of the Dead *30*
Bourani, Greece 78, *79*
Brassempouy, Landes, France 8, *12*
Breuil, Abbé 14
Brewster, Earl 110
Britannicus 152
brothels 126–7, *126, 127, 128*
Bubastis (Zagazig) 41
burial mounds *20*

Caesar, Julius 137–9, *137*, 154
Caesar-Augustus, Emperor 17
Caligula, Emperor 127
Calvert, Frank 50
Canopus canal *162*, 169
Capitoline hill, Rome 118
Capitoline Venus (*callipygous Venus*) *146*, 149
Carnarvon, Earl of 38
Carrara 140
Carter, Howard 38
cartouches 35, 42
Carystios *102*
Cashford, Jules 16
Casius, Mount 160
Cassandra 120
Cato the Elder 130, 134
Catullus, Gaius Valerius 134
cave paintings 12, 14–15
Celer, Metellus 134
Cephisus 72
Cerne Abbas Giant, Cerne Abbas, Dorset *8, 20*, 21
Chadyr, Russia 18, *18*
Chaeronea, battle of 68
Cheremisin, Dimitri 17, 18
children 17
Christianity 160
Christie Painmter 95, *95*
Cicero, Marcus Tullius 135, 137, 138, *154*
Cinyras 91
circumcision 29, 160
Claudius, Emperor *152*
Cleis 85
Cleopatra 138, *138*, 139, *139*
Cnidian Venus *see* Aphrodite of Knidos

Colosseum, Rome 149, 150
Commodus, Lucius 165
Constantine, Emperor 170
contraception 40–41
copulation 15
Corinth 62, 77, 130, 157
courtesans 74
creation 27–8, 30, *32*
Crete 44–8, 59–60
Cumae, Campania, Italy 118, *118*, 120
Cumaean Sibyl 118, *118*, 120, 170
Cupid 58, 118, 133, *135*, 146, *149*, 150
Cyclops 59
Cypriot script *52*

Daphnis *100*
death 97
Deir el-Bahari, Upper Egypt 35, *35*
Delilah 29
Delos island 99, 102, *102*
Delphi 159, *159*
Demosthenes 105
dildos *84*
Dimitian, Emperor 152
Diogenes 99
Dione 58
Dionysus 56, *58*, 77, *84*, 101–2, *102*, 120, 162
divorce 40
Dordogne region, France 14, 15
Dying Gaul statue (Epionos) 137, *137*

Earth Mother/Mother Earth 59, 72, 170
Echo 72, 73, 99
Egyptians 30–42
    contraception and extramarital attitudes 40–42
    gods and goddesses 30–33
    people and everyday life 38–40
    the sexual conduct of the pharaohs 34–8
Eighth Paylon, Karnak *37*
'Amarna 37
Eleusian mysteries 159
Ellanodikai (Olympic judges) 71, 72
Eos 95, *95*, 96
Epaminondas 68
Ephesus 78
Ephesus, Turkey 140
Ephorus 47
Epiktetos from Anzi *82, 84*

Epionos *137*
Erechtheum, Athens *162*
erections 90, *91*
Erim, Professor Kenan 140
Erixymachus 57, 64–5
Eros 58, *63*, 92, *93*, 94, 118, 130, 133, *170*
eros 58, 62
Etruscans 110–17
Eurydice 117
Evans, Sir Arthur 44, *49*
'evil eye' 110, *115*, 123
Ezekiel 29

'family of Chadyr' 17–18, *18*
fauns *102*
fellatio *126*
female cult 52
female goddess, decline of 22, 24, 52
fertility cults *10*
festival of Adonis 91–3
Fischler, Dr Susan 143–4
Fitzgerald, Professor William 146
Flammian Priests *143*
Fort-Harrouard, France *10*
French Pyrenees 11
fresco wall paintings 44, *44*, 48
Freud, Sigmund 38
Frying-pan or Ring, Cerne Abbas *20*

Gaia 59, 72
Galba 156
Gannymede *55*
Garden of Eden 28
Geb (earth god) 30, *30*
Giza great pyramid 35
gladiators 146, *150*
goddess of love 16–17, *17*, 41
Golden Fleece 97
Grave Circle, Mycenae *51*
Great Pyramid of Khufu, Giza *138*
Greece
    hetairai, courtesans and prostitutes 74–8
    homosexuality and the law of Athens 73–4
    the rise of Athens 52–60
    self-love and the story of Narcissus 72–3
    Sparta, sex and sport 67–70
    the tomb of the diver and a colonial symposium 65–7
    the two types of love 60–65
    'Where Burning Sappho Loved and Sung' 82–5
    women and the Games 71–2
    see also Athens
Greek statues 7
Grimaldi, Italy *10*

Grotte de Lascaux 14
group sex 77
Gulf of Corinth 139
gymnasia 68, *71*, *73*, *74*

Hadrian, Emperor *152*, 156–70
Hadrian's Villa, Tivoli *161*, 162, *162*, *165*, 166
Hagar 29
Halicarnassus 88
Hammurabi, King of Babylon 22, 24, *24*, 27
Harmodius 63, *63*
Hathor (goddess of love) 30, 32, *32*, *33*, *33*, 41
Hathor's temple, Dendera 41–2
Hatshepsut, Queen 34, 35, *35*, 37
Haute-Garonne *11*, 12
Hebron 27, 29
Helen of Troy 48, 50–51
Hera 52, *55*, 71, 101, 117, 118
Hercules *112*
Hermaphroditus 79, 81, *81*, *84*
Hermes 77, 79, *84*, 97, 99, *99*, *118*
herms 97, *99*, 104, 105
Herodotus 25–6, 41, 44, 96, 117
Herophile 118
Hesiod 59
hetairai 56, 74–5, *82*, 88, *92*, *93*
    see also prostitution
High Priestess of Demeter 72
Hipparchus *63*
Hippias 63, *63*
Hissarlik hill 50
Hittite Empire 26
Homer 50, 51, *51*, 59, 68, 96
Homo sapiens 8
homosexuality 63, 67–8, *71*, 72, 73–4, *81*, 134
    see also lesbianism
hoplites 104
Horace 121
horse sacrifice 26
Horus (sky god) 32–35, 37, *170*
'House of Venus', Pompeii *123*
Hyperides 75

Ihy *33*
incest 26, 32, 34
Ionia 63
Isaac 29
Ishtar (goddess of love) 25
Isidora 162
Isis 30, 32, 33, *35*, 37, *170*
Israelites 29–30
Isturitz, France 14, *14*

Jason 97
Jerusalem 29
Jezebel 29
Joseph 29
Judaism 27–8

Julia (Pompey's wife) 137, 138, 144, 145, 154
Juno 110, 118
Jupiter 118, 159
Juvenal 146

Kallicrates *69*
Karnak 35, *37*, 42
Keijl, Van *72*
Kephalos *95*
Keuls, Professor Eva 63–4, *78*, 104, 106
'King Priam's Treasure' 50–51
Knidos 77
Knidos, Asia Minor *60*
Knossos royal palace, Crete 44, *44*, 47
Kos island 77
kottabos (a game) 66, *92*
Kronos 59, 60

'The Lady of Mycenae' *44*
Laetoli, Tanzania 7
Lake Bikal, Siberia 11
Lascaux cave complex 12
Laussel, Dordogne 15, 16, *16*
Lawrence, D. H. 110, *110*, 112, 113, 115
Le Mas Capelier, Averyon *12*
Leakey, Louis 7
Leakey, Mary 7, 8
Leonidas, King of Sparta *105*
lesbianism 82–5
Lesbos (now Mitylene) 82
Lespuge *11*, 12
Leto *99*
Levkas island *86*
libation ceremony 97
Little Palace, Knossos 48
Livia, wife of Augustus 143, *143*, 144
Livy 127–8
Love in the Ancient World (film) 90
'Lupanara' brothel, Pompeii 126–7, *126*, *127*, *128*
Lysippus 133, *133*
Lysistrata (Aristophanes) 88, 90, *90*, *91*, 105

Macedonia 93, 130, 133
Maenads 97, *102*
Magdalanian period 14, *14*
Maia *84*, 97
male cult 52
Marathon 52
Marduk (Babylonian god) 22, 24
marriage 24–5, 34, 39–40, 88, 137, 144
Mars 118, 149, *149*, 157, *157*
Marshack, Alexander 10
Mas d'Azil, France 14, *14*
Mausoleum of Halicarrnassus 96

May Day-Maypole dance rite *20*, 78, 79
Meaden, Dr George 20
Medea 97
Medusa the Gorgon 97
megaliths 18–19
Memphis 162
Menelaus, King of Sparta 48
menhir statues *12*
Mentuhopte II, Queen *38*
Mercury *118*, *154*
Mesopotamia 22, *22*
Messalina 152
Metella, Clodia 134, 135, 137
Michelangelo 120
Miles, Christopher *90*
Miles, Suzy *26*
Minerva 118
Minoans 44–8, *44*
Minos, King of Crete 44
Minotaur 44, 49
moon 16–17, *17*, 19
Mortuary Temple of Hatshepsut, Deir el-Baharai *35*
mosaics 58, *154*
Moses 29
Mother Goddess 19, 20–21
Mount Ida 60
Mount Olympus 52
'Munchner Lekythos' 97
music 41–2, *100*, *101*
Mycenae 44, *51*
Myrrha 91, 93

Nammu (Babylonian goddess) 22, 24
Napoleon Bonaparte *162*
narcissism 72–3
Narcissus 72, *72*, 73, 99
Neanderthals 8
Nefertiti, Queen 7, 37, *37*
Nephthys 30
Nero, Emperor 152, *152*, 154, 156
Nestor, King 48
Nicias 105
Nike *64*
Nile River 162, 167
Norwich, John Julius 140, 142
Nut (sky goddess) 30, *30*, 32, *32*
'Nutcracker man' 7

Obelisk to Antinous, Rome *169*
Octavia, Empress 152, 154
Octavian, Emperor 139
Oedipus complex 38
Olduvai Gorge, Tanzania 7
Olympia 63, 77
Olympic Games 68, 71, 72, 156
Oppian Law 130, 134
Original Sin 28
Orpheus 117
Osiris 30, 32, 162

175

Osyppus of Megara 68
Ovid (Publius Ovidius Naso)
  145–6, 149, 150

Paestum *64*, 65
Palace of Nestor, near Pylos 48, *48*
Palaeolithic art 15
Pallas Athene 55
Pan *63*, 97, 99, *99*, *100*, 102, 126,
  170
Pandateria island 144, 154
Panourgia, Maria *90*
Paris, son of King Priam 48
'La Parisienne' 44, *49*
Parmenides 59
Pasiphae 149
patriarchal system 29
Paul, St 159
Paulus, General Aemilius 130, 133
Pausanius 57, 60, 62, 64, 65, 71
Pausias *101*
Pavlidou, Alexandra *90*
Peloponnese *99*
Penthesilea, Queen 96
Pericles 55, 57, *60*, 74, 75, 85, *104*
Persephone *50*, 91–2, *92*
Persia/Persians 52, 63, 105, *105*
petroglyphs 17, 18
Phaedrus 57, 58, 59
phallic symbol 97–102
    for good luck 121, 124–6,
    124
Phaon *86*
pharaohs 34–8
Pharos lighthouse, Alexandria 139
Pherenike 71
Philip, King of Macedon 68
Phryne *60*, 75
Piette, Edouard 8, 10
Pincio hill, Rome 169, *169*
Pius, Antoninus 165–6
Plato 55–6, *55*, 57, *57*, 58, *58*, 63,
  64, 65, 67, 68, 77, 79, 81–2, 83,
  86, 94, *104*
Platonic love 63
Plautus 137
Plutarch 68, *96*
polyandry 22
polygamy 29
Polyzalus of Gela *156*
Pompeii 121–7, 146, *150*, 152, *152*
Pompey (Gnaeus Pompeius
  Magnus) 137
Poppaea (Nero's mistress) 152, 154
Poseidon, temple to, Paestum *55*
Pothinus the Eunuch 138–9
Praxiteles *60*, 75, 77, *84*
Priam, King 51
Priapus (god of fertility) 120–21,
  120, 123
'Priest-King' 44
'Prince of the Lilies' (fresco) 47

prostitution 26, 41, 56, 62, 74, *74*,
  75, 77–8, *81*, 116, 117, 126–7,
  128, 144 *see also* hetairai
Psyche 133, *135*
Ptolemy XIII 138–9
Ptolemy XIV 139
pyramids 19, 30
Pythian Games *156*

Ra (sun god) *32*
Radio Carbon Accelerator 18
Ramesses II *42*
Ramesses III *42*
Ramses II temple, Hir-wer 162
Reeder, Dr Ellen 88, 92, 93
reggio di Calabria 144
Rhea 59–60
Rhodes island 71
rites of passage 12
rock carvings 14, *15*, 16, 17
Rockwell, Peter 130, 133
Roman Mammisi, Dendarah
  complex *33*
'Roman orgies' 127–8
Rome
      and Greek culture 130
      women of 130–39

Sabina, Emperess 156, 157, *157*,
  165, *166*
Salamis, battle of 52
Salmacis 79
Samson 29
Sappho 82–5, *85*, 86
Sarah (Abraham's half sister) 29
satyrs 99, 101, *102*
Scheil, Jean Vincent 22
Schliemann, Heinrich 50–51
Schliemann, Sophia 51
'Sebasteion' monument,
  Aphrodisias 17
Semele 56, *58*, 101
Seneca 144, 152, 154
Senenmut *35*
Sergeac, Dordogne *15*
Seth (god of disorder and
  confusion) 30
Seven Wonders of the Ancient
  World 96, 139
sexual conduct, laws of 24
sexual deviations 29
Shakespeare, William 8, 138
shaman 12
Sheba, Queen of 29
Shu (god of the air) 30, *30*
Sibyls 118, 120
Sicily 104, 105
Silbury Hill, near Avebury 19–20,
  19, *21*
sileni 101
Silenus *100*, 101, 102
Siphnos *99*

Sirius 37
Sistine Chapel, Rome 120
'Skira' ritual *78*
Skopas Minor *149*
snake-goddesses 44
Socrates 56–7, *56*, 74, 85–6, *104*
Solomon, King 29
Solomon's Temple, Jerusalem 161
Sophocles 38
South Altai, Russia 17
Sparta/Spartans 60, 63, 67–8, *69*,
  88, 105, *105*
sphinx *38*
stele *22*, 24
Stoa of Eumenes *57*
Stoibadeion, Delos 102, *102*
stone circles 20
Stonehenge 18–19
Susa *22*
Sybaris 65–5
Symposium 56
Symposium (Plato) 56, 58–9, 64–5,
  68, 77, 79, 86, *104*
Syracuse, Sicily 105
Syrinx 99

Tarquin I, King of Rome 118
Tarquinia 110
Tefenet (goddess of moisture) 30
Temple of Aphrodite, Aphrodisias
  60, 63
Temple of Aphrodite, Corinth 77
Temple of Apollo, Corinth *133*
Temple of Apollo, Delphi *156*
'Temple of Dionysos' *see*
  Stoibadeion
Temple of Hera 71
Temple of Isis, Delos *170*
Temple of Mars, Rome *149*
Temple of Mut, Rhebes *30*
temple prostitutes 26
Temple Repositories, Knossos 44
Temple to Olympian Zeus *160*
Tennyson, Alfred, Lord 169
Thebes 37, 38, 68, 162
Thebes, King of 101
Theocritus *99*, *100*
Theopompus 115–17
thermae 154
Thermopylae pass *105*
Theseus 44, 47, *49*
Thoth ('lord of the divine words')
  33, *35*
Throne Room, Knossos *47*
Thucydides 108
Tiberius, Emperor 144
Titans 59
Tithonos 95, 118
Titus, Emperor 160
Tiy 37
'The Tomb of the Bulls' *110*,
  112–13, *112*, *113*, *115*

'Tomb of the Diver' *64*, 65–7,
  65
'Tomb of the Jugglers' *215*
'Tomb of the Leopards' *4*, 113
Tomb of Nakht, Thebes *40*
Tomb of Nebamun, Thebes *40*
tomb paintings 42
'Tomb of the Whipping' fresco
  116
Tomi, Black Sea 145
Trajan, Emperor *33*, 156, 157
transvestites *78*
Troilus *113*
Trojan War 48, 50, 96
Troy 51
Turk, Dr Ivan 8
Tutankhamun 7, 37–8
Tuthmosis I, Pharaoh 35
Tuthmosis III, Pharaoh *33*

Uni 110, 118
Ur 27
Uranus 52, 58, 60, 62
Urukagina, King 22

Varsami, Constantina *90*
Venus 118, 149, 157, *157*
Venus de Milo 7
Venus figurines 10–12, 15
'Venus with the horn' 16
'Venus' of Laussel, Dordogne *16*
'Venus' of Lespugue,
  Haute-Garonne *11*
'Venus' of Willendorf *8*, 10
Vesuvius, Mount 123, *123*, 152
Villa Mirenda, Scandicci *110*
Virgil *118*
Vulci 94
vulva imagery 14–15, *15*

Walters Art Gallery, Munich 88
weddings 39, 67–8, 94
West Kennet Long Barrow 19, *20*
West, Mae 40–41
women
      in Athens *see under* Athens
      and the Olympic Games
      71–2
      of Rome 130–39
women, attitude towards 28–9
writing 22

Xenophon 77–8
Xerxes *105*

Yahweh 26, 27–8, 29
Yazilikaya 26

Zeus 52, *55*, 56, *58*, 59, 60, *69*, 81,
  82, *84*, 91, 92, 95, 97, 99, *99*,
  101, 117–18, 159, 160, 161
Zinjanthropus boisei 7